ASPEN PUBLISHERS

A Practical Guide to
Legal Writing
& Legal Method

Third Edition

Teacher's Manual

John C. Dernbach
Cathleen S. Wharton
Joan M. Ruhtenberg
Catherine J. Wasson

Wolters Kluwer
Law & Business

AUSTIN   BOSTON   CHICAGO   NEW YORK   THE NETHERLANDS

ACKNOWLEDGMENTS

Paula Heider and Kimberly Peterson provided superb secretarial support on this project. Robert Altenburg, Widener University School of Law Class of 2008, provided valuable editorial assistance. And of course, we thank the thousands of students who constantly inspire us to find new and better ways to teach.

SUGGESTIONS OR COMMENTS

If you have suggestions or comments about the text or this teacher's manual, or about teaching with these materials, please contact us:

John C. Dernbach   jcdernbach@widener.edu
Cathleen S. Wharton   wharton1@uga.edu
Joan M. Ruhtenberg   jruhten@iupui.edu
Catherine J. Wasson   cwasson@widener.edu

CONTENTS

Part A
INTRODUCTION TO LAW

Part B
BASIC CONCEPTS OF LEGAL METHOD

Part C
BASIC CONCEPTS OF LEGAL WRITING

Part D
THE OFFICE MEMORANDUM

Part E
BRIEFS

APPENDICES

ABOUT THE THIRD EDITION

The third edition of *A Practical Guide to Legal Writing & Legal Method* retains the practical, process-oriented approach to teaching Legal Writing and Legal Method that has been the hallmark of this text since the first edition of the book was published in 1981. Accordingly, the structure and purpose of the book remain unchanged. We continue to offer students a straightforward guide to the essential skills of legal reasoning, analysis, and communication that they will use every day in their practice of law. The third edition, however, expands and updates the material to suit the needs of a new generation of law students and law professors.

For those of you who have used earlier editions of the book, major changes from the second edition are highlighted below. More detailed information appears at the beginning of each chapter. For those of you who are new to the book, we believe that you will find a wealth of ideas to help you become the best teacher that you can be. Like its predecessors, the third edition is easy to teach with. It does not require teachers to adopt a particular teaching style or adhere to a specific pedagogical philosophy. Rather, it provides a flexible framework that encourages teachers to make creative, thoughtful choices about their work in the classroom and allows legal writing teachers to amend, supplement, and expand each lesson to meet the needs of their own students. Whether you are a new or a returning user of *A Practical Guide*, we hope that the third edition provides your students with the opportunity to learn and practice the skills they need and that this Teacher's Manual supports you in your teaching.

Major Changes From the Second Edition

<u>Coverage</u> – The third edition contains new or expanded sections on several topics, including the structure and operation of legal rules, case briefing, synthesis, describing the law, and the organization of a legal discussion or argument.

<u>Exercises</u> – Exercises have been updated when appropriate. Additional exercises have been added to several chapters.

<u>Appendices</u> – The Appendices have been updated and revised. In the second edition, the appendices included an office memorandum and trial briefs on one case, and an office memorandum and two appellate briefs on a different case. The appendices to the third edition, however, follow a single case, *Tyler v. Eastern Pacific University*, from an objective office memorandum all the way through the appeal. The second sample office memorandum on *Tyler v. Eastern Pacific University* (Appendix D in the second edition), has been replaced with a sample trial court order, while the two appellate briefs (Appendices E and F), present the parties' arguments on appeal of that order. Appendix G has likewise been updated to include some excellent new resources on writing style and grammar.

<u>Teacher's Manual</u> – The teacher's manual for the third edition has been expanded significantly. Users will find additional teaching suggestions for many chapters, and many additional exercises that can be used in lieu of or in addition to the exercises in the main text. Several new Appendices have been added, including annotated examples and grading criteria for several exercises and assignments.

<u>CD for the Third Edition</u> – The teacher's manual is also available on CD for teachers who have adopted *A Practical Guide* for use in their classes. The CD contains all of the exercises in the text and the entire teacher's manual. It also contains Appendices D, E and F from the second edition of the text. Professors can examine text or critique examples in class using document readers or Smartboard™ technology, print and copy exercises for classroom projects, and edit or adapt exercises and other materials to suit their own course goals and teaching needs.

INTRODUCTION

The best part of teaching with *A Practical Guide* is that the book works. From week to week, month to month, we have seen substantial (if not always consistent) progress from the overwhelming majority of our students. At the end of the year, they are much better writers than they were at the beginning.

Teaching with *A Practical Guide* requires a commitment to three pedagogical principles. The rest is up to the teacher. These principles are as follows:

> ➢ Legal writing is taught most effectively when it is taught together with legal method. Writing about a specific hypothetical problem gives students an extended opportunity to think deeply about that problem. Most of the hypothetical problems in other first-year classes are answered orally and during an individual class; writing an answer over a period of days and weeks reinforces and deepens students' ability to think like lawyers. Legal writing is not English composition for lawyers. Rather, it is perhaps the only course that brings together the entire law school curriculum.

> ➢ Legal writing and legal method involve at least several dozen discrete basic skills. These skills are best taught several at a time and sequentially, with the most fundamental skills first.

> ➢ These skills are learned best by practicing them in exercises. A considerable amount of research, and much experience with the book, indicates that people learn more by doing than by simply listening or taking notes.

Although we care deeply about these principles, there is no one right way to teach with the book. Each teacher enriches *A Practical Guide* with his or her own experience, ability, and personality. For the beginning legal writing teacher, this manual provides specific suggestions. The experienced legal writing teacher may find some of these suggestions elementary. For those teachers, however, this manual also provides points of departure.

The materials in this manual reflect this diversity. Suggested answers or approaches were written by different authors, and reflect differences of emphasis, teaching style, and professional experience. When an exercise requires drafting of a statement of facts, discussion, or other element, moreover, the manual shows preliminary steps but frequently not the final written product. The book shows a good deal of our writing. We encourage you to show students other writing (yours or theirs). Finally, the suggested answers or approaches in the book are not necessarily the only answers or approaches. In many exercises, you might analyze or resolve a problem differently.

Teaching with This Book

In our experience, the principles, explanations, and examples in the chapters require little or no additional explanation in class. Students usually have no difficulty understanding what they are reading. As a result, we spend a few minutes at the beginning of class answering questions or emphasizing one or two points, but we do not lecture from the book. Instead, we spend our time where the students are likely to experience problems—applying what they have read to specific situations. Most of the class time with this book, therefore, involves the exercises.

There are many exercises from which to choose. The book contains more than sixty exercises that are identified as such (*e.g.*, Exercise 11-B). With a little imagination, you can create many more. The exercises are based on several dozen factual situations. You could take a factual situation illustrating one skill (such as common law analysis) and use it again to illustrate another skill (such as writing questions presented in a memorandum). In some cases, the book uses the factual situations that way, but in many cases it does not. You can also use the ideas behind the exercises to create your own.

Work through an assigned exercise yourself before you go over it in class. This manual contains answers to some of the exercises and a method of approaching the answers to others. It should go without saying that you should not use that as a substitute. We have found that we understand an exercise better if we have worked through it first. It is difficult to answer some questions in class unless you have worked through the exercise beforehand.

As you work through an exercise, decide what you want to emphasize. Each exercise can be taught in different ways and can be used to focus on different points. In addition, decide how the exercise can be made most useful for the writing problem that you have assigned the class. The exercises, of course, are not a substitute for memo- or brief-writing assignments. But they can and should be used to give students practice in the skills they will need to demonstrate on those assignments.

Similarly, when you assign an exercise, make sure you emphasize to students the importance of working through the exercise before class. We suggest to students that they come to class with their notes from this work. Over and over, we tell them that they will be well rewarded for the time they spend working on an exercise out of class. Sometimes, we use incentives and penalties to ensure that they do.

In teaching any exercise, you have several choices:

Classroom discussion vs. hand-in assignment. Classroom discussion works well for many of these exercises. It is usually a pretty good way to get across the basic points made in the chapter. The dialogue (Socratic and otherwise) that you have with students will be helpful to many of the other students. The disadvantage is the one that occurs in any class—some students prepare and some do not.

One way to solve this problem is to require students to type their answers to the exercises and turn them in after class. You (or your research assistant) can then review the answers, determine whether they are adequate, and place a mark in the grading book for those who did not turn in the assignment or who turned in exceptionally poor work. The paper is not graded; it is merely reviewed to see whether the work was done. Of course, you could always use this review to identify common problems.

The exercises can also be used for hand-in assignments. Whether they are graded or marked on a pass/fail basis, this is obviously a good way to ensure that students actually do the exercises. Requiring written answers is almost never an adequate substitute for classroom discussion of the exercise, however. Reading and marking the papers can also overwhelm you, particularly if you have large classes or give many of these assignments. Too many written assignments can also overwhelm students.

Another option, particularly for lessons that you believe deserve additional emphasis, is to have a classroom discussion of an exercise and require students to turn in written answers to the exercise for the next class.

<u>Role-playing.</u> Role-playing works extremely well for the exercises in Part E (Briefs). But it can also work well for other exercises, even exercises involving objectivity and memo writing. If we plan to take a role-playing approach to an exercise, we typically tell half the students in the class to prepare as if they represented Party A in the exercise, and the other half to prepare as if they represented Party B. When they get to class, we have them answer questions from their party's point of view. If a student representing Party A makes a certain point, we might ask a student representing Party B to answer it. Then we might ask the Party A student to respond.

Role-playing is a particularly effective way of making certain points that are difficult to make in other ways. You might use it, for example, to emphasize objectivity in memo writing by having students representing opposite sides assess the strength of their client's position. A similarity in views about a particular party's position would suggest objectivity. A substantial difference in views would suggest lack of objectivity or perhaps ambiguity in the law.

Role-playing also increases student interest and participation. In our experience, students feel more engaged when they are pretending to be someone's attorney and recommending or advocating something. It is also fun to teach this way.

<u>Peer review.</u> Another way to increase student interest and performance is to require each student to give his or her paper to one or more other students at the beginning of class. They can critique the other student papers in small groups, or you can have students talk about other student papers in a classroom discussion. Peer pressure is often (although not always) a means of improving performance. We have found that students are very interested in the work done by their peers. To keep the discussion focused, you should identify the criteria you expect students to use (*e.g.*, the signposting principles in Chapter 13), or give them a checklist of tasks to accomplish during the review process.

If you base a classroom discussion on other student papers, however, you should encourage your class not to criticize other students by name. Students are sensitive to criticism of their work; if you teach more than one section, consider swapping samples for in-class critiques. Some professors adopt a code system for peer review projects.

An effective means of peer review is to hand out three to six papers (more or less) to the entire class. These papers, from which names have been omitted, are labeled by number or letter. The teacher then asks specific questions about Paper A or Paper B. Students get to see good and bad examples of the particular points being taught. These papers can be pulled from a pile of hand-in assignments, or certain students can be required to turn in the assignment in advance. If the second route is chosen, it may be important to require that all students turn in an assignment early sometime during the semester or year.

Using the Appendices

The appendices in the text are good teaching tools, particularly as students are writing memos or briefs, because they show the entire document. The negligent misrepresentation problem in the appendices is essentially an elements problem. This problem is very much like those that first-year students encounter in their other courses.

Additional appendices are included in the teacher's manual. These include annotated sample discussions based on some of the exercises in the text; a section of one section of Appendix A in the text, annotated to show organizational principles at work; and a sample grading/criteria sheet.

Part A
Introduction to Law

1
Rules and Policies

Changes From The Second Edition

There are no major changes from the second edition. A minor change is that the cases in Exercise 1-B have been rearranged, to progress from the easiest questions to the more difficult ones.

Teaching Notes

This chapter is a good introduction to law school in general and legal writing in particular. We have found that the chapters in Part A can also be useful in preliminary or orientation classes for first-year students.

Suggested Approach To Exercises

These exercises work well as a basis for class discussion during the first or second class. The discussion is often lively. Assigning written answers to one of the exercises after class discussion is an easy introduction to legal writing because students are writing about ideas already explored in class.

Exercise 1-A

1. Because the questions involve the extent to which a government ought to regulate the activities of its citizens, the answers should be consistent with the balance that the students strike between the common good and individual liberty. Encourage students to develop these questions:

    ► Is the harm to be prevented great enough to justify the intrusion on individual liberty?
    ► Is the harm to be prevented great enough to justify the cost to enforce it?
    ► Is there a proven connection between the harm and the remedy? (Will the remedy work?)
    ► Is the remedy practical, in the sense that it will have sufficient public support to be enforceable?

2. One way to explore consistency is to ask students questions about the views implicit in their answers to 1. Their "gut" views about the bills in 1 may reveal a more complex understanding of freedom and the social good than they have previously stated. Some students will argue, for example, that freedom from wearing motorcycle helmets is different from and less important than the freedom from government-sponsored testing before getting married.

3. This question is intended to encourage students to think about the tension between philosophical consistency and political necessity. In a democratic society, the public (and therefore the voters) may not want consistency. Legislators are expected to be principled *and* responsive—a tension that is not always easy to resolve. Judges are expected to be principled but are not expected to respond to public demands. Thus, it is probably more important that judicial decisions be consistent.

Exercise 1-B

1.   **(a)**   No. Price's guilt or innocence does not depend on what crimes the other men committed.

     (b)   No. That other people violated the same law does not excuse Fong's violation. Even though her arrest might seem arbitrary, it is related to the purpose of the law, which is to enforce speed limits on the highway.

     (c)   No. That other people violated the same law does not excuse Hyde's violation, even though she was arrested "at random." Her arrest "as an example to others" is consistent with the purpose of discouraging the use of marijuana.

     (d)   Probably. It is no defense that the cohabitation law has not been enforced against others in recent years. However, if Gilman can show that her arrest was not made in good faith but in an attempt to intimidate her into silence, she has a valid defense. On these facts, she can probably make that showing.

2. It is no defense that the defendant was arrested at random, that other persons breaking the same law at the same time were not arrested, or that the law had not been enforced in the past, unless the defendant can show intentional discrimination in enforcement. See the cases listed in the Bibliography.

2
Sources of Law

Changes From The Second Edition

We added a list of states and territories within each federal judicial circuit and changed Exercise 2-B.

Teaching Notes

This chapter is the cornerstone of much that you will be teaching. We recommend assigning it early as an overview of our system of laws and coming back to it as you teach specific principles of legal method. If you also teach legal research, this chapter is a good starting place.

Students will have no difficulty recognizing binding authority and secondary authority. They will not agree on the relative merits of persuasive authority, and the disagreement gives you an opportunity to discuss the value of each source. Realistically, they might use all of the cases listed.

Students may also have difficulty when they have a larger number of cases to choose from and cannot decide which ones to use. Before the first research memo, suggest the following guidelines:

In general, choose cases as follows:

(1)   For a question of state law, prefer state court over federal court decisions.

(2)   Prefer a case with similar facts over one with dissimilar facts.

(3)   Prefer a case in which the court addressed the specific issue in your case over one where the issue was more general.

(4)   Prefer a case with a well-reasoned basis for the decision over one where the rationale is superficial or nonexistent.

(5)   Prefer decisions of a state's highest court over decisions of its middle level appellate court.

Balance these preferences with your own judgment and common sense. For example, a well-written and well-reasoned federal district court opinion on a question of state law might be more useful than a state court decision on the same issue. If you have kept an open mind during your research, the cases most helpful to you in analyzing and resolving the issues will usually be the ones most helpful to the reader.

Suggested Approach To Exercises

Exercise 2-A

       Category (A)—primary authority that is binding: 1, 5.
       Category (B)—primary authority that is persuasive: 3, 4, 6, 7, 8.
       Category (C)—secondary authority: 2.

   (1)   Sources 6 and 7 are most persuasive for two reasons: (1) This is a matter of state law, and the court will look at how other state courts have resolved a similar issue of state law before they look at federal court decisions. (2) They are decisions by the highest court of the respective states.

   (2)   Source 3 is better authority than source 4, the federal case, because it is a decision by a state court on a question of state law. The federal court in Source 4 necessarily based its decision on a prediction of how the highest court in that state might rule on the identical issue.

   (3)   Source 8 has the least precedential value because it is a minority opinion, not a holding.

Exercise 2-B

       Category (A)—primary authority that is binding: 7.
       Category (B)—primary authority that is persuasive: 3, 4, 5, 8, 9.
       Category (C)—secondary authority: 1, 2, 6.

This exercise presents a situation in which many of the decisions on a question of contract law, traditionally the province of the states, have been decided by federal courts trying to ascertain state law. This exercise also emphasizes a concept that students sometimes lose sight of—that federal courts cannot make state law. Sources 8 and 9 are examples of the same court reaching different conclusions based on the state law it was construing.

   (1)   Sources 3 and 5 are both highly persuasive. Source 3 is a case nearly on point on a matter of state law decided by the highest court of another state. Source 5 is an opinion from a federal trial court judge applying the law of your state. A state court would be very interested in how a federal court applied that state's law.

   (2)   Sources 8 and 9 have some persuasive value because they are cases in which the federal court had some state law upon which to base a decision, though Source 9 is slightly more persuasive because the court was relying on a decision by the state's highest court.

(3)   Source 4 has less precedential value than the other sources because it is an opinion from a federal judge deciding an issue without any guidance from the courts in that state.

This exercise serves as a good example of the importance of developing an overview of the law before narrowing your research to the most persuasive sources. You could explain to students that only after reading the secondary sources and some of the cases would they have discovered that the courts are in disagreement as to whether the pollution exclusion clause applies only to traditional environmental pollution, such as industrial discharge of pollutants into the air and water, or whether it also applies to a contaminant released inside an enclosure. Once the students realized this distinction, they would concentrate on cases involving indoor releases, such as those listed in the exercise.

3
Case Analysis and Case Briefs

Changes From The Second Edition

We added a sixth element, "Disposition," to the case briefing format and included a fuller explanation of procedural facts. The example and explanation of a case of first impression and the chart showing the elements of a case brief of *State v. Jones* are also new. Other changes are minor.

Teaching Notes

To the extent that you rely directly on our suggested answers to the exercises , you may want to emphasize that there is room for discussion about some of the elements. The purpose of any case brief is to provide the person writing it with a concise and accurate summary of the case. This can only be accomplished if the writer learns to read cases carefully and think about them critically. You can encourage students to focus on the substantive content of a case rather than on the format of their case brief by pointing out that the text <u>does not</u> instruct them to develop the elements of a brief in the order in which those elements will appear in the final product. Rather, the text tells students to identify the fourth element, the holding, first. Students then work backwards from the holding, identifying the essential elements of the case as they go. We encourage each student to develop a style of case briefing that he or she finds most helpful. Students' increased use of computers makes it much easier for them to construct a case brief in the order suggested in the text, or in any other order that suits them, even though the elements of the final brief are typically presented in a different order.

Several elements of a case brief can be difficult for students. For example, if the court does not explicitly identify them, it is not always clear which facts are legally significant. It can be helpful to point out that courts often reiterate the facts that they deem most significant either immediately before or immediately after the holding. Also, students may find it helpful to list the legally significant facts and the procedural history of the case separately, as illustrated by the alternative case briefing format and sample brief below. Another difference in the alternative format is that it requires students to include both the significant facts and the legal question in the issue statement (thus anticipating the questions presented element in a memo, as explained in Chapter 19), so that the holding can be stated as "yes" or "no."

The difference between rules and reasoning or policy may be particularly difficult for students to discern. Generating a discussion about what your students included in their briefs, where they placed certain information and why, and how their brief compares with those of their classmates enables you to illustrate how two different answers may both be accurate and helpful. Explaining their answers will also help the students to define and understand these elements more clearly.

Some teachers find it helpful to have student's brief longer cases after briefing some or all of the cases in these exercises. Longer cases that we have found useful for that purpose include those cited in the Bibliography for Exercises 13-A and 14-A. Obviously, teachers who use these or other cases in the bibliography for case briefing find that students are more familiar with the law when they subsequently do the exercises. Another source of cases for practice is the materials in the "closed" memo projects that you might assign fairly early in the semester. The immediate and obvious usefulness of this work can be a powerful motivator for students.

Finally, you might tell your students that although all lawyers must be able to identify the essential elements of a case, there is more than one format for a case brief. Some lawyers combine the facts and procedural history; others do not. Some combine the holding and the disposition; others do not. Some put the parts of the brief in a different order. You could encourage your students to focus on the content of the brief rather than on its formal structure by giving them an example of an alternative format, such as the one below:

Alternative Format for a Case Brief.

I.   **Heading**. Include the name of the case, the court that decided the case, and the date.

II.   **Facts.** Include all facts directly relevant to the issue. Relevant facts include the relationship of the parties to each other and a summary of the occurrences giving rise to the litigation. It saves time to use abbreviations such as Pl for plaintiff, D for defendant, TC for trial court, and so forth.

III.   **Procedural history.** Explain how the court below decided the case and why the decision was appealed.

IV.   **Rule.** State the rule–the legal principle that applies to the facts of the case.

V.   **Issue or issues.** State the substantive question or questions the appellate court decided. A statement of an issue includes (a) the point of law in dispute and (b) the key facts relating to that point of law.

VI.   **Holding.** The holding is the court's answer to the question presented in your issue statement. If your issue statement is complete, the answer can be "yes" or "no."

VII.   **Disposition.** State whether the court affirmed or reversed the lower court's decision and whether the appellate court remanded the case to the trial court for further proceedings.

VIII.   **Reasoning.** Explain the reasoning of the court in reaching its decision.

IX.   **Comments.** This section is for your benefit. Include here any points you want to remember that were not included in other sections.

Sample Case Brief

State v. Phillips

Facts: D set fire to a building and the building burned to the ground. A fireman on his way to the fire was killed when he fell off the truck and was run over by a car. The driver of the car was speeding and following too closely.

Procedural History: D was convicted of arson, which is a felony, and felony murder. She appealed the felony murder conviction.

Rule: If someone is killed during the commission of a felony, the perpetrator of the felony is guilty of felony murder.

Issue: Is D guilty of felony murder when a fireman fell off a truck and was run over by a speeding motorist while the fireman was on his way to the scene of an arson that D had committed?

Holding: No.

Judgment: Reversed.

Reasons: The purpose of the rule, which is to deter people from committing felonies inherently dangerous to human life, would not be served in this case. D could not foresee that an intervening force, a third party, would cause the death of a fireman. There must be a causal connection between the felony and the death.

Comment: The court noted that because felony murder borders on strict liability the scope of the crime should not be expanded beyond its intended purpose.

Suggested Approach To Exercises

Exercise 3-A

Toad v. Ulrich (2002)

<u>Facts</u>: The plaintiff sells wooden stools called "Toad Stools" at a roadside stand. The defendant sells similar stools from another roadside stand and has advertised them as "Toad Stools." When the defendant began selling his stools, the plaintiff asked him not to use the name "Toad Stools." Even though the defendant continued to do so, the plaintiff took no further action until he filed this lawsuit for trademark infringement two years later. The trial court awarded damages and granted the plaintiff an injunction. The defendant appealed.

<u>Rule</u>: If a person does not actively defend his trademark against known infringements, including the bringing of a lawsuit if necessary, a competitor is free to use the trademark after two years.

<u>Issue</u>: Did the plaintiff actively defend his trademark?

<u>Holding</u>: Yes. Asking the defendant not to use the name "Toad Stools" was sufficient for a small businessman to actively defend his trademark.

<u>Disposition</u>: Affirmed.

<u>Reasons and policies</u>: Small businesses have fewer resources than large businesses and should not be held to the same standard. The smaller the business, the easier it should be to satisfy the active defense requirement.

Exercise 3-B

Bronson v. Road Runner Shoe Co. (1976)

<u>Facts</u>: The plaintiff was injured when struck by a truck owned by the defendant and driven by one of the defendant's employees. The employee was on his way back to work after visiting his girlfriend during his lunch hour. He had not been given permission to use the truck, but normally he had sole possession of the keys during working hours. The company had never objected to his private use of the truck. The plaintiff sued the defendant under the theory of *respondeat superior*. The trial court granted the defendant's motion for summary judgment, and the plaintiff appealed.

<u>Rule</u>: An employer is liable for the torts of its employees when they are acting within the scope of their employment.

<u>Issue</u>: Was the employee acting within the scope of his employment?

Holding: Yes. Even though the employee did not have permission to use the truck during lunch, he was acting within the scope of his employment while he was driving back to work.

Disposition: Reversed.

Reasons and policies: Because employers have control over their employees, employers are responsible for the torts their employees commit. Employers cannot avoid such responsibility by asserting that the actions of their employees were not authorized; few employers actually authorize employees to commit tortious acts.

Exercise 3-C

State v. Phillips (1999)

Facts: The defendant set a building on fire. While on the way to the fire, a fireman was killed when he fell off the truck and was run over by a car that was speeding and following too closely. The defendant was convicted of arson, a felony, and felony murder. She appealed from her conviction for felony murder.

Rule: If someone is killed during the commission of a felony, the defendant is guilty of felony murder.

Issue: Is the defendant guilty of felony murder?

Holding: No. The defendant cannot be held criminally liable for the death of the fireman from an unforeseeable risk, even though it occurred during the commission of a felony.

Reasons and policies: The felony murder rule is intended to deter people from committing felonies, especially those that are inherently dangerous to human life. Holding a defendant responsible for a death from an unforeseeable risk created by an intervening force would not further that purpose. There must be a limit to the nearly strict liability imposed under the felony murder rule.

4
Precedent and *Stare Decisis*

Changes From the Second Edition

There are no major changes from the second edition. The only minor changes are an increase in the dollar amounts in Exercises 4-C and 4-D.

Teaching Notes

Exercises 4-A, 4-B, and 4-C work better as vehicles for discussion than as writing assignments because the concepts of precedent and *stare decisis* need considerable exploration in the classroom. Exercise 4-C also gives you a chance to introduce an idea that will be developed in Chapter 24 (Briefs to a Trial Court): trial courts are reluctant to depart from established law in the jurisdiction.

Class discussion of Exercise 4-D can take well over an hour because it is difficult to develop precise rules in a large group. We have had success dividing the class into small groups of five or so, with each group working through the exercise and one member of each group recording the answers. We then had the answers typed and distributed them during the next class meeting. You could also require written answers to Exercise 4-D and use the best ones as a basis for class discussion.

Some professors have worked through some of the exercises in this chapter in the context of a motion argument. For exercise 4-A, for example, students would be assigned to represent Fowler or the insurance company and instructed to prepare an argument based on the only relevant authority, *Eckersly*. This, of course, requires one party to interpret the precedent more broadly and the other to interpret it more narrowly. If you like, you can assign three students to sit as a panel of judges. While the "lawyers" develop their arguments, the "judges" must prepare one or two questions for each side. After the argument, the judges can decide the case and explain their decision.

The need to actually argue the case, rather than discuss it in the abstract, helps many students understand that "the law" is elastic and that there is not always a single "right answer" to every question. This kind of hands-on approach is a good teaching technique for the experiential learners in your class. It can also invigorate students who came to law school eager to argue a case, only to discover that they must spend hours every day reading and briefing cases and being told that the answer to every question is "it depends."

Suggested Approach To Exercises

Exercise 4-A

1.	The court has jurisdiction to hear Fowler's case because the insurance company did not obtain service by trickery or fraud. This case is unlike *Eckersly*, where the plaintiff secured service of process by resort to what the court termed "shocking fraud." The plaintiff in *Eckersly* obtained service of process by luring the defendant, an out-of-state resident, into the state with a false story that his mother was terminally ill. The plaintiff in this case did not lie in order to entice Fowler into the state. Fowler entered the state voluntarily in order to satisfy a merchant's potential claim against her. Although the merchant who served the papers on Fowler secretly worked for the insurance company, his failure to disclose that fact was not fraud or trickery because there was no misrepresentation.

2.   The result is fair because Fowler submitted to jurisdiction by entering the state voluntarily and because the defrauded insurance company will now have the opportunity to prove its case in court without resort to fraud or trickery to obtain service of process.

3.   *Eckersly* could also support a decision for Fowler. That the merchant was a secret employee of the insurance company suggests subterfuge. Collusion between the merchant and the insurance company to entice Fowler into the state might be trickery because the merchant did not tell Fowler about his dual role, but it would probably not be fraud because there was no active misrepresentation.

Exercise 4-B

1.   Yes. Even though the later case did not mention *Waterford*, the definition of reckless endangerment set out in *Waterford* is no longer accurate. Operation of a motor vehicle in violation of the law is still reckless operation as set out in *Waterford*, but after *Seperic*, the reckless operation must also endanger the lives or safety of others in order to constitute reckless endangerment. This is an example of implicit overruling, although the *Waterford* decision is still helpful in defining reckless operation of a motor vehicle.

2.   Students may find support for either conclusion. How they explain and support their decision is more important than how they decide the case. Some (but not necessarily all) points students might make:

Conviction affirmed:

Under *Waterford*, Buckler's violation of the provision that prohibits driving while under the influence of alcohol establishes that his operation of his vehicle was reckless. Not only is there an analogy to be made regarding the collision that each driver had, but there is also an analogy in that both drivers were under the influence of alcohol. Further, the *Seperic* requirement that the reckless operation endanger the life or safety of another seems to be satisfied because Buckler was not only driving after drinking heavily but also was doing so with a passenger in his car. Drunk driving in our society has come to be synonymous with endangering the lives and safety of others.

Conviction reversed:

It is difficult to conclude beyond a reasonable doubt that Buckler violated the provision prohibiting drunk driving; he was not charged with that violation, so it was not proved at trial. Thus, it is questionable whether, under the definition of reckless conduct given in *Waterford* and *Seperic*, his conduct can be so characterized. The type of accident that occurred in *Waterford* is distinguishable from that which occurred here. In *Waterford* the driver actually ran down the decedent. Here, the accident occurred when Buckler's car left the road. There is no indication as to why it did so; thus, there is no evidence to show beyond a reasonable doubt that he was operating his car in a manner that endangered anyone's life or safety.

Exercise 4-C

1. Under the only binding case on point, Elson would not be entitled to a refund. In *Aaron*, the court reaffirmed the difference between a land contract and a mortgage. Because Elson chose to purchase her land under a land contract, she "risked losing everything." The buyer in *Aaron* had only paid about one-third of the purchase price before the default and Elson had paid approximately three-fourths. The *Aaron* court's reasoning, however, does not seem to leave this avenue of distinction open.

    In an appellate setting, *Deal* could be used to try to persuade the court that the difference between land contracts and mortgages is more form than substance and that treating the two transactions differently is unfair. Elson could even argue that under the concurring opinion, she should recover. The concurrence reaffirms the difference between these two types of contracts, but opens the door for equity to step in. Here, because Elson has paid so much of the purchase price, she has a very strong argument in equity. But students need to realize that *Deal* is only persuasive and, as such, has a limited impact on this decision.

2. Students may disagree as to whether this is fair. Elson, as an elderly blind woman who stands to lose everything, will likely generate a good bit of sympathy. Some students, however, may look at the problem from the perspective of the mortgage company and reason that the mortgage company went into this transaction with certain expectations and that it is not fair to change the rules at this point. You may find it helpful to designate groups of students to represent each side and let them take turns arguing their position.

3. Students should be able to see how the cases could be used to argue the other side: a fairness and equity argument for Elson and a fairness and legal argument for the mortgage company. But emphasize again the different precedential value of these two cases.

Exercise 4-D

1. Yes, Tubbs can collect the money. If the terms in a written contract are fully negotiated and understood by the parties, the contract should be enforced as it is written. In this case, Hoffman agreed to pay full price for the stereo even if it was damaged in transit.

2. Various forms of this problem have been reported in the news in the wake of Hurricane Katrina in 2005.

    (a) Yes, she can recover. The terms of a policy should be negotiated and the parties informed of all pertinent terms. The insurance company did not discuss flood insurance with Goldberg or tell her that flooding was not covered in the policy.

An exclusion in the middle of a seven-page document is not an acceptable substitute for full discussion of the terms of the contract.

(b) No, she cannot recover. The terms of the policy were set out in the contract and agreed to by both parties. Goldberg had a duty to read the contract and discover what she was contracting for. At the least, she had a duty to ask whether damage from flooding was covered, or whether coverage was available. The contract was not fully negotiated only because Goldberg chose not to negotiate.

(c) Answers will vary. It is important that students be able to explain their decisions.

3. **(a/b)** No, the dealer cannot collect the remaining amount. The application of the rule that a contract fully negotiated by the parties should be enforced is unfair in this situation because Graff did not have the knowledge or sophistication to negotiate or even understand the terms of the contract.

(c/d) Yes, the dealer can collect the remaining amount. Graff agreed to the contract price. Unlike the Goldberg case where the seller hid a pertinent provision in the middle of a seven-page contract, the seller in this case explained what Graff had contracted for—$30 per month for the next five years. The contract is not void simply because the buyer lacked the skills to compute the total price of the refrigerator.

(e) Answers will vary. It is important that students be able to explain their decisions.

Part B
Basic Concepts of Legal Method

5
Understanding Legal Rules

Changes From the Second Edition

This chapter and the exercises in it are new.

Teaching Notes

This chapter acts as a bridge between Parts A and B of the text and helps students make the transition from thinking about the law in a somewhat abstract way to using the law to solve specific problems. At the most essential level, a student's ability to understand how the law is "put together" will determine whether that student's analysis of a problem is strong or weak, compelling or unpersuasive. You can use the lessons in this chapter to further two important teaching goals: (1) to help students become more careful readers; and (2) to begin to show students the connection between the structure of the law, issue identification, and the organization of a written legal discussion or argument.

How Rules Are Constructed

Many students have trouble parsing rules thoroughly. Many more have trouble with complex rules, or have trouble transferring their understanding of a rule into an organizational framework for the analysis of a legal issue. At whatever point your students get stuck, you can help them by showing them how to make a "picture" of a legal rule. Several examples appear below. Consider having students work in small groups to create a visual depiction of the rules in the chapter exercises, using a variety of the methods shown below.

Many students find the elements charts used in Chapters 6 through 8 in the text helpful; you might ask students to look ahead to see how those are constructed. Students with strong verbal skills and linear thinkers may prefer to create an outline. Visual and experiential learners might prefer a more abstract representation, such as the "modules" shown below. Students with scientific and mathematical skills might prefer a flow chart. Whatever they prefer, it is important for students to understand that there is more than one way to study and more than one way to organize legal information. Every year some students find that the penny drops when they see information presented in an atypical way. The examples below are based on the Restatement (Second) of Torts § 13 (1965), which is discussed in the text and reads as follows:

An actor is subject to liability to another for battery if

(a) he acts intending to cause a harmful or offensive contact with the person of the other or a third person, or an imminent apprehension of such a contact, and

(b) a harmful contact with the person of the other directly or indirectly results.

Outline – This is a fairly typical rule outline. You can easily show students how to adapt this outline for their Torts class by weaving examples from key cases into the outline where appropriate.

A defendant is liable for battery if:

I.   The defendant acts

II.   With intent to cause:
     A.   A harmful contact <u>or</u>
     B.   An offensive contact <u>or</u>
     C.   An imminent apprehension of a harmful contact <u>or</u>
     D.   An imminent apprehension of an offensive contact

III.   With either of the following:
     A.   Another person <u>or</u>
     B.   A third person <u>and</u>

IV.   Harmful contact with the other person results either:
     A.   Directly <u>or</u>
     B.   Indirectly.

Modules – This is an unusual approach, but every year the light seems to go on for at least one or two students when they see a rule illustrated in this way. The approach was developed by a student when she was asked to list all the things that related to the defendant's intent, then to the defendant's target, etc.

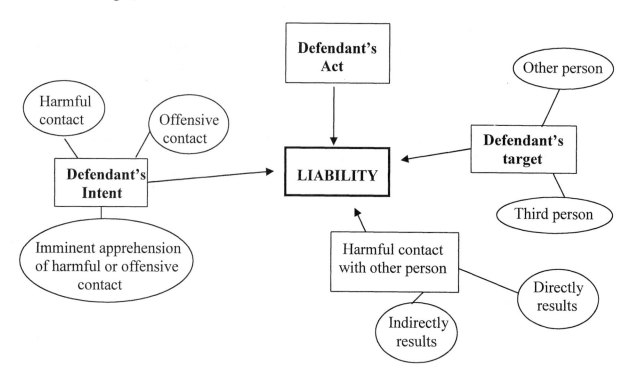

Flowchart

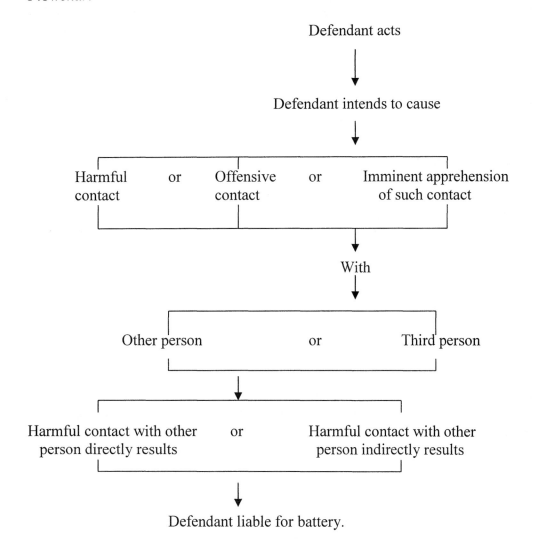

Defendant acts

↓

Defendant intends to cause

↓

Harmful contact   or   Offensive contact   or   Imminent apprehension of such contact

↓

With

↓

Other person   or   Third person

↓

Harmful contact with other person directly results   or   Harmful contact with other person indirectly results

↓

Defendant liable for battery.

     Visual depictions of the law will provide valuable information about how to structure the written legal analysis of any issue.   A lawyer—or law student—who understands the workings of a rule so well that she can design a vivid, detailed "picture" of the law will know exactly what steps must be taken to resolve a legal question.

<u>Developing a Rule from Multiple Sources—Synthesis</u>

Students often have a difficult time teasing out relevant factors from a series of cases. If you discuss the hate crime cases in this chapter in class, you can show students how to look for common characteristics in a series of cases. At the same time, you can restate an important point about reading the law. A typical judicial decision begins with an overview of the facts of the case. Not all of those facts will turn out to be relevant, but the court will often repeat selected facts shortly before it announces its holding on a particular issue. Remind your students that if the court thought those facts were worth repeating, they should probably pay attention because these are the most relevant facts, the facts upon which the court relied in reaching its decision.

It can be helpful to have students look at two or three cases to demonstrate this point. Consider finding some of the hate crime cases that formed the basis for one of the examples in this chapter. You could also look at cases that your students are using for a closed memo, or find examples in a casebook from one of your students' other classes. The lesson to take away is this: whether you are briefing a case for Property or trying to synthesize cases, if you are not sure which facts matter, start with the facts that the court mentions more than once.

Suggested Approach to Exercises

Exercise 5-A

This is a fairly simple starting place because the rule as written identifies the three elements of the rule. Consider reminding students, however, that the punctuation of a rule, including enumerations like those present in this example, does not always tell the whole story. In the Restatement (Second) of Torts example in the text, for example, more than one element or sub-element appears in some of the clauses (<u>e.g.</u>, "a harmful contact with the person of the other directly or indirectly results").

1.   The rule contains three elements: The first element describes requirements for the testator, the second element describes the requirements for the beneficiary, and the third element describes the benefit received by the beneficiary.

2.   The first element has two requirements—the testator's intellectual capacity and the time at which that capacity is measured. Both must be present or a will could be voided if the testator was perfectly competent when he executed the will but was of weakened intellect at death.

3.   The rule is conjunctive—all elements must be present.

4.   Undue influence "sufficient to void the will" is established.

5.   The result if the elements of the rule are established is not entirely clear. If the showing is "sufficient to void a will," does it follow that the will <u>must</u> be voided? Ask students to consider the possibilities to try to arrive at an answer. Assume, for example, that a court decides not to void a will for undue influence. Which is more likely: (1) The court concluded that there was insufficient evidence of undue influence. (2) The court concluded that there was sufficient evidence of undue influence, but decided not to void

the will. This exercise presents a perfect opportunity to tell students that the law will not always provide them with a definitive answer to every question. Sometimes they will need to rely on their common sense—just as they did before starting law school.

Consider taking some time here to discuss the benefits and drawbacks of the various kinds of rule consequences. Firm consequences have the benefit of being clear and uniform, but they can be rigid and unresponsive to unique circumstances. Discretionary rules, on the other hand, are flexible and allow a judge to shape the rule to fit the circumstances of an individual case. That same flexibility, however, makes it difficult to predict how the rule might be applied in a given situation, and can lead to uneven results.

6.   No exceptions.

Exercise 5-B

This is a good example to discuss in class because it allows you to work through some common errors that students make when they are learning to read the law. First, students often fail to distinguish between elements or sub-elements, and as a result they paint with too broad a brush and miss important details. In this example, students may make assumptions based on the punctuation of the rule and think of "extreme and outrageous" as a single concept. Students should be asked to consider whether it is possible for conduct to be "extreme" but not "outrageous," in which case an element would not be established. Conversely, students sometimes chop a rule into too many small pieces that cannot stand on their own. In this rule, for example, students often separate "intent" from "toward the plaintiff." Intent, however, has little meaning standing alone; one cannot simply "intend." Intent requires a focus; one must intend <u>something</u>. In this example, students must understand that the defendant's intent must not simply be present; it must also be directed toward the plaintiff. Finally, this example allows you to discuss causation—the mere presence of a defendant's intentional behavior toward the plaintiff and the plaintiff's distress is not enough; there must be a causal link between the two. Some further explanation of this exercise follows:

Intentional Infliction of Emotional Distress (IIED)

To establish intentional infliction of emotional distress, the conduct of the defendant must be intentional toward the plaintiff, the conduct must be extreme and outrageous, there must be a causal connection between the defendant's conduct and the plaintiff's mental distress, and the plaintiff's mental distress must be extreme and severe.

1.   The rule contains four elements if you divide the rule as punctuated—the rule has four clauses, all of which require something. It contains seven elements if you consider the pairs of ideas embedded in three of the clauses.

2.   See above.

3.   This is a conjunctive rule. All elements and sub-elements must be present.

4. The defendant is liable for IIED.

5. Mandatory. The words "to establish" imply that the result <u>will</u> follow if the elements are established.

6. No exceptions in the rule as presented.

Exercise 5-C

This exercise allows you to once more focus on the importance of critical reading as you work through the parts of the rule with your students. Some points for discussion include the following:

1. The case concerns a minor, not an adult.

2. It is not enough that the bar <u>served</u> a minor, the rule requires that the bar "know or should know" that the person served is a minor.

3. The risk of harm to another must be an <u>unreasonable</u> risk—what might that mean?

4. The risk of harm must also be foreseeable—make sure your students notice that the court includes the fact that the tavern employees knew that Cooper was going to drive.

5. One can infer from the facts of the case and the court's decision that there has to be a causal connection between the foreseeable risks and the actual harm that results.

The rule from *Nicholson v. Carson's Tavern* can be broken into several elements. A typical outline of the rule from the case might look like this:

A tavern is negligent if:

1. It sells alcohol
2. To one who it knows or should know is a minor **and**
3. Thereby creates a risk of harm to others that is:
   a. Unreasonable **and**
   b. Foreseeable **and**
4. The minor causes injury to another.

Exercise 5-D

One way to handle this exercise, especially if it is your students' first attempt at synthesizing a rule from a series of cases, is to ask students to do a depiction of the rule from each case first, then blend the elements together into a rule that encompasses all of the cases. You might want to explain that this is an inductive reasoning process: one uses a series of specific examples to create a general rule. Possible examples of rule depictions from the three cases, and a synthesized rule of the four cases together, follow:

Teniel v. Olde Towne Inn – this case expands the rule from *Nicholson* in two ways: (1) it applies the rule to people who are obviously intoxicated, and (2) it applies the rule to injuries to the intoxicated person.

A tavern is negligent if:

1.   It sells alcohol
2.   To one who it knows or should know is intoxicated **and**
3.   Continues to serve the person **and**
4.   It is reasonably foreseeable that the person could harm himself or others **and**
5.   The person causes injury to himself.

Valerio v. Glenn – This case expands the rule in *Nicholson* by extending its reach beyond licensed sellers to social hosts.

A social host is negligent if:

1.   The host serves excessive amounts of alcohol
2.   To a guest that the host knows is a minor guest **and**
3.   Injury to another is reasonably foreseeable **and**
4.   The intoxicated minor injures another.

A synthesis of the rule as developed through *Nicholson*, *Teniel*, and *Valerio* might look something like this:

A person is negligent if:

1. The person is a holder of a liquor license **or** a social host, **and**
2. The person sells or furnishes alcohol
3. To someone that the person knows or should know is:
   a. Intoxicated **or**
   b. A minor **and**
4. The provider of the alcohol creates a risk that is:
   a. Unreasonable **and**
   b. Foreseeable **and**
5. The intoxicated person thereby injures:
   a. Himself **or**
   b. Another.

When your students have synthesized the three cases, you can point out that rules do not just tell us what the law <u>is</u>. Rules also help us to identify what the law has <u>not</u> said. Ask your students what the synthesized rule does <u>not</u> tell us—*i.e.*, what questions remain unanswered? The court's reasoning in *Valerio*, for example, makes it unclear whether the case will apply to adult guests as well as to minor guests. Similarly, it is not clear whether *Valerio* changed the rule as it applies to minors: must the defendant merely "serve" a minor (*Nicholson*), or serve "excessive amounts" (*Valerio*)? Finally, all of the cases deal with injuries due to drunk driving. Would other kinds of behavior by the intoxicated person be deemed foreseeable? What kinds of behavior, and why or why not?

Additional Exercises

If you use the additional exercises below you (and your students) will undoubtedly notice that the facts and law for Exercise 5-E are very similar to *State v. Klein*, used in Chapter 3. The example in Chapter 3 focuses on the common burglary element of "entry" into a building to teach students how to articulate the holding in a judicial opinion. In contrast, the exercise below presents the element of "entry" in the context of a complete burglary statute, then asks students to consider how that element has been defined or interpreted in two different cases. The exercise below thus gives students the opportunity to practice a more difficult skill in a somewhat familiar setting.

Exercise 5-E, below, is also somewhat similar to an additional exercise for Chapter 6, Exercise 6-C, which also analyzes authorities on burglary. The statutory rule in Exercise 5-E, however, does not require a "breaking," while the common law rule in Exercise 6-C does. If you use both of these examples with your students, we suggest that you remind them that the definitions of many crimes and causes of action differ from state to state.

Exercises 5-F and -G, below, are similar to an example in Chapter 12; both involve the shopkeeper's privilege defense to a suit for false imprisonment. The exercises below ask students to synthesize a statute and two cases to determine what the rule is. Chapter 12 uses the same subject matter to show students how to explain the law in context: although the example focuses on the shopkeeper's defense, the text reminds students to explain that the defense only arises in the context of an alleged shoplifter's suit for false imprisonment.

Using different versions of a rule, or applying the same rule to different fact scenarios, can help students learn to think more flexibly and more critically by encouraging them to revisit familiar material for different purposes. As students become more familiar with an area of law, you can expect them to demonstrate a deeper understanding of the law and to work with it in a more sophisticated way. On a more practical level, if you have limited in-class time with your students, this technique allows you to spend a little less time making sure that students understand the law on which an exercise is based and a little more time on the particular skill being taught.

Exercise 5-E

Your supervisor has asked you to do some research for a burglary case she is defending. You are particularly interested in discovering the meaning of the word "enter" as used in the statute.

The relevant law consists of a statute and two cases:[1]

Section 137.02 Burglary

A person is guilty of burglary if he enters a building or occupied structure, or separately secured or occupied portion thereof, with intent to commit a crime therein, unless the premises are at the time open to the public or the actor is licensed or privileged to enter.

State v. Mathers (1984)

Defendants appeal their conviction for burglary, arguing that the evidence was insufficient to establish all elements of the charge. We affirm.

The state's only witness was Al Szymanski, a security guard for the Garden Hill school district. At approximately 6:15 p.m. on November 11, 1980, a school holiday, Mr. Szymanski was notified of a possible break-in at Garden Hill High School. He went to the scene and found Defendants inside the high school, removing laptop computers from one of the computer labs. Some plywood that had been used to board up a broken window had been removed, and the lock on the door to the computer lab had been broken. Defendants were arrested and charged under § 137.02, which provides in pertinent part that a person is guilty of burglary if he "enters" a building with intent to commit a crime inside.

Defendants argue that there was no proof that they had "entered" the building because there was no evidence that they removed the plywood from the broken window. Although it is true that the plywood could have been removed hours before the security guard arrived, proof of "entry" does not require proof of a breaking-in; it is sufficient to prove that any part of the body of the intruder entered the premises. Because Defendants were apprehended <u>inside</u> the school, they clearly had "entered" the building. Affirmed.

State v. Holloway (1993)

Defendant appeals his conviction for burglary of a sporting goods store. He argues that the evidence does not establish a prima facie case of burglary because no part of his body entered the store. We disagree.

The parties stipulated to the following facts: Police responded to a silent alarm at All Sports Xtreme. When they arrived, they found a jacket sleeve protruding from the mail slot in the store's front door. A straightened coat hanger was on the ground near the door. The store's owner told police that several knitted caps had been taken from a rack inside the store, near the door, but there was no evidence that the store had been broken into. Defendant was apprehended at a gas station near the store with the stolen caps in his possession. He admitted that he had used the coat hanger to pull the caps through the mail slot in the door. He also admitted that he had attempted to remove the jacket, but it was too bulky to fit through the slot. Defendant then abandoned the attempt and fled the scene.

---

[1] This exercise is based on 18 Pa. Cons. Stat. Ann. § 3502(a) (West 2002); *Commonwealth v. Gordon*, 477 A.2d 1342 (Pa. Super. Ct. 1984); and *Commonwealth v. Peterson*, 21 Pa. D. & C. 4th 222 (1993)

The obvious purpose of the burglary statute is to protect the sanctity of the building and the safety of the persons and contents within it. When that building is penetrated by an offender with the intent of committing an offense, in this case theft of the owner's goods, it does not matter whether the entry was by the defendant's entire body, by defendant's hand or arm, or by an instrument held and manipulated by those body parts. We therefore hold that the entry into the store only by the instrument of the coat hanger, under the facts of this case, constitutes an "entry" under our present burglary statute.

Write a statement of the rule on "entering."

* * * * *

You can use this exercise as either a homework assignment or an in-class exercise. Ask your students to draft their own rule, or have them draft the rule with a partner. You can then collect and critique all of the various versions of the rule that your students create. In the alternative, hand out the following sample rule statements (Answers A and B) and ask students to critique each one. You can begin the discussion by reminding students what the supervising attorney has asked for. Then ask which statement of the rule the supervisor will find most helpful and why.

ANSWER A: A person is guilty of burglary if he enters or gains access to a building in any way with intent to commit a crime. Section 137.02; *State v. Mathers; State v. Holloway.*

ANSWER B: A person is guilty of burglary if he enters a building with intent to commit a crime. Section 137.02. The element of entry can be established in two ways: (1) if the defendant uses any part of his body to enter the premises, *State v. Mathers,* or (2) if the defendant holds and manipulates an instrument with his body to gain access to the premises. *State v. Holloway.*

Both answers cite all of the relevant authorities. Answer B is better, however, because it states the rule on entry with absolute clarity. The reader knows immediately that the element can be satisfied in two different ways and can easily check the rule against a new set of facts to see if the element is met. Answer A is much weaker. It implies that there is more to the word "enter" than meets the eye, but the phrases "gains access to" and "in any way" are too vague to be of much use to the reader.

Exercise 5-F

You work in the legal department of a large chain of hardware stores. Your supervisor asked you to find the "shopkeeper's privilege" statute.[2]

---

[2] This exercises is based on Ga. Code Ann. § 51-7-60 (1998).

§ 15-60-7. Shopkeeper's Privilege

Whenever the owner or operator of a mercantile establishment or any agent or employee of the owner or operator detains, arrests, or causes to be detained or arrested any person reasonably thought to be engaged in shoplifting and, as a result of the detention or arrest, the person so detained or arrested brings an action for false imprisonment against the owner, operator, agent, or employee, no recovery shall be had by the plaintiff where it is established by competent evidence:

(1)   That the plaintiff had so conducted himself or behaved in such manner as to cause a man of reasonable prudence to believe that the plaintiff, at or immediately prior to the time of the detention or arrest, was committing the offense of shoplifting; and

(2)   That the manner of the detention or arrest and the length of time during which such plaintiff was detained was under all the circumstances reasonable.

1.   How many elements does this rule contain?
2.   Do any of the elements have sub-elements?
3.   What type of rule is this—disjunctive, conjunctive, a factors test, a combination of types?
4.   What result if the elements of the rule are established?
5.   Is that result mandatory? Prohibited? Optional or discretionary?
6.   Are there any exceptions to the rule? If so, when do they come into play? What result if an exception to the rule exists?

The shopkeeper's privilege can be asserted as a defense to a false imprisonment claim. It is therefore, conceptually, a kind of exception to the general rule on false imprisonment. You can show students how the defense arises by starting with the definition of false imprisonment: "the unlawful detention of the person of another, for any length of time, whereby such person is deprived of his personal liberty." Ga. Code. Ann. § 51-7-20 (1998).

You can then begin this exercise by working through the elements of false imprisonment: (1) detention of another, (2) for any length of time, (3) that is unlawful, and (4) deprives the person of his or her personal liberty. The shopkeeper's privilege relates to the third element because if the defendant is "privileged" to detain the plaintiff the detention is not "unlawful." After laying this foundation, you can then work through the remainder of the exercise with your students:

1.   The rule contains six elements: Merchant – detains person – person reasonably thought to be shoplifting – person sues for false imprisonment – person's behavior would lead a reasonable person to believe that person detained was shoplifting – detention was reasonable.

2.   This rule can be confusing to work through because students get bogged down in the details. Focus their attention by asking students to identify the basic topics covered by the rule: (a) the merchant, (b) the act of detention, (c) the alleged shoplifter, and (d) the nature of the detention. Then you can work with students to identify obvious sub-elements. For example, one can use the general term "merchant" to include owner,

operator, agent, and employee; "detain" includes detain, arrest, cause to be detained, or cause to be arrested. Then you can discuss the nature of the detention—it must be based on a reasonable belief that the person was shoplifting, and it must be reasonable in manner and duration. Now there are only a couple pieces still unaccounted for. There is some overlap between the requirement in the first paragraph of the rule, that the merchant "reasonably thought" that the person detained was shoplifting, and the requirement in subsection (1) that a "reasonably prudent" person would believe that the person was shoplifting. The two concepts, however, are not precisely the same. The remaining requirement that the person detained sue for false imprisonment is an additional element.

3.   It has a combination of conjunctive elements and conjunctive or disjunctive sub-elements.

4.   The detainee cannot recover for (or the merchant is not liable for) false imprisonment if the elements of the rule are established.

5.   The result is mandatory: "no recovery shall be had."

6.   There are no exceptions to the rule. As mentioned above, the statute itself can be characterized as an exception to the general false imprisonment rule.

Exercise 5-G

Review the shopkeeper's privilege statute in Exercise 5-F   Then read the case summaries below[3], and create a synthesized rule using the statute and both cases. In what ways does the synthesized rule differ from the original rule that was based on the statute only?

Kovarik v. Big Box Stores, Inc. (1986)

The Appellant, Dan Kovarik, commenced this action for false imprisonment and intentional infliction of emotional distress after being questioned by his employer regarding the theft of store merchandise. The trial court dismissed the false imprisonment claim, and Kovarik appeals.

Kovarik worked as a kitchen designer for Big Box Stores. In March 1984 he was summoned to the store security office and questioned for two hours about reports from coworkers that he was stealing store merchandise. Kovarik testified that he agreed to talk with the guards and signed a consent form. During the subsequent interrogation, two guards took turns questioning him, leaving three- to five-minute intervals between the interrogation sessions. Kovarik was also allowed to go to the rest room (accompanied by a male security guard) and spent about thirty minutes writing at statement. Kovarik testified that both guards called him a liar, and one guard slammed his hand down on the desk and shouted while questioning him. He admitted, however, that he did not complain to the

---

[3] Cases in this exercise are loosely based on *Crowe v. J.C. Penney, Inc.*, 340 S. E. 2d (Ga. Ct. App. 1986); and *Jackson v. Kmart Corp.*, 851 F. Supp. 469 (M.D. Ga. 1994).

guards and did not ask to stop the interview. In fact, Kovarik admitted that he preferred to continue the interview "to clear everything up."

The trial court found that the reports from Kovarik's coworkers that he was stealing store merchandise furnished probable cause for him to be questioned under the shopkeeper's privilege statute, § 15-60-7. The court found further that the defendant was privileged to reasonably detain Kovarik to investigate the matter. Finally, the court found that Kovarik was not detained against his will. We agree. Kovarik signed a consent form before the interview and at no time did he request that the questioning be stopped. Indeed, he testified that he wanted to remain to "clear everything up." Under these circumstances, it cannot be said that Kovarik was "detained," as he was not held against his will. The trial court did not err when it dismissed Kovarik's false imprisonment claim.

Williams v. Southern Exposure, Inc. (1997)

Marcia Williams sued Southern Exposure, Inc. for false imprisonment after being detained on suspicion of shoplifting by a security guard employed by the store. Southern Exposure's motion for summary judgement was granted by the trial court and Williams appeals. We reverse and remand the case for trial.

Alex Gallacher, a security guard, suspected that Williams was placing small items of clothing in her purse as she shopped at Southern Exposure, an upscale boutique. Gallacher shadowed Williams until he clearly saw her slip an expensive scarf into her purse and then followed her to the checkout desk. Williams paid for a sweater, but she did not remove any other items from her purse to pay for them. Gallacher stopped Williams as she left the store and asked her to produce her receipt and empty her purse. When Williams refused, Gallacher grabbed her by the arm and led her to an office in the back of the store. He locked the door and told Williams that she should "cooperate" with him because he could "do whatever he wanted" and no one would believe a "thief and a whore" if she complained. Williams immediately agreed to cooperate and gave the scarf and two other items to Gallacher. She then signed a statement admitting that she had engaged in shoplifting, and was allowed to leave the store. The detention lasted no more than ten minutes.

The court found that Gallacher had probable cause to suspect Williams of shoplifting. It found further that although Gallacher subjected Williams to "gratuitous and unnecessary indignities," the ten-minute detention was so brief that the detention could not be considered unreasonable. We disagree.

It is clear that Southern Exposure had probable cause to suspect Williams of shoplifting. Her behavior aroused the suspicions of Gallacher, who followed Williams until he personally witnessed her place store merchandise in her purse and leave the store without paying for it. The reasonableness of the detention, however, is not simply a question of minutes or hours. The reasonableness of the length of the detention may be impacted by the manner in which the person is detained. Although Williams' detention only lasted about ten minutes, Gallacher's abusive language and thinly veiled threats of physical or sexual assault could allow a jury to find that the detention was unreasonable in both manner and duration. We therefore reverse and remand for a trial on the merits.

Each case adds something to our understanding of the rule. *Kovarik* helps to explain two elements: (1) what kinds of facts support a "reasonable belief" that someone was shoplifting, and (2) what "detain" means. Some students may want to discuss whether the guards' behavior during Kovarik's detention—yelling, pounding on the table—was unreasonable or, conversely, whether the fact that Kovarik was given breaks means that his detention was reasonable. This allows you to reiterate the importance of critical reading of authorities and provides you with a good opportunity to discuss accuracy in case description and interpretation. Can one draw conclusions about the meaning of these facts when the court did not rely on them to reach its conclusion? The court did not dismiss Kovarik's claim because it concluded that the detention was reasonable. It dismissed the claim because the employee <u>agreed</u> to be questioned; the detention was not "against his will." Without that element, the claim fails, regardless of the reasonableness or unreasonableness of the detention. (Of course, Kovarik might be able to pursue additional claims— <u>e.g.</u>, for battery or emotional distress, if the facts supported those claims. Remind students that they must focus on and answer the question asked.)

Williams helps to explain what kind of conduct will cause a court to conclude that a detention was not reasonable in manner or duration. Be sure that students understand that there is no specific time period that is "too long;" even a relatively short detention can be unreasonable if the manner in which the person is being detained is egregious enough.

6
Identifying and Selecting Issues for Analysis

Changes From the Second Edition

We changed the jurisdictional amount and the amount of medical expenses in the *Brookson* problem in the text and the dollar amounts in Exercise 6-A.

Teaching Notes

There are no additional notes for this chapter.

Suggested Approach to Exercises

Exercise 6-A

The factual and legal materials for this exercise are also used in Exercises 9-A, 11-A, and 12-A.

The problems faced by first-year law school teachers generally—where to begin and how to judge student work based on their imperfect knowledge of how to find and ascertain the "law," how the legal system works, and how to analyze legal issues—are particularly acute in legal writing courses. We require written analysis early, before they have much acquaintance with substantive law, while they are still learning to read and brief cases, and before they have read the succeeding chapters in this book on how to organize and write about legal issues. You can use this exercise to preview principles used in later chapters.

We have used this exercise not only as an exercise in deriving and applying rules of law from cases to spot issues but also as an exercise in preparing to draft a discussion using common law analysis. As a class exercise, the students outline the tentative issues, find and state the rules that apply, parse the rules, and fill in the outline with the specific issues and sub-issues that arise from the rules. They also list under each issue or sub-issue (1) the relevant facts of this case, (2) the relevant facts and holding of the precedent cases, (3) any analogy or distinction that could be drawn between this case and precedent cases, (4) reasonable inferences from (1), (2), and (3), and a conclusion. From this class outline, the students can draft a paper that includes most of the requirements described in later chapters. Some of us hand out an annotated sample discussion of the offer issue and then require students to write a discussion of the acceptance issue. Annotated discussions of these two issues can be found in Appendices A and B of the manual.

This early introduction to the structure and content of a legal analysis, via this exercise or another, is critical for those courses that require papers before Part C (Basic Concepts of Legal Writing) is covered in full.

This exercise is also useful as a review of Chapter 2 (Sources of Law), with emphasis on the precedential value of concurring opinions, dissenting opinions, and secondary authority.

Finally, this exercise introduces two kinds of legal issues. For offer and acceptance, the question is "How does the law apply to the facts of this case?" For consideration, the question is also "What is the law?"

1.   To have a valid contract, there must be (1) an effective offer, (2) a valid acceptance, and (3) sufficient consideration.

    (1)   For an offer to be effective, the offeror must intend to make a binding contract. The test for intent is whether a reasonable person in the offeree's shoes would believe that the offeror so intended.
    (2)   To be valid, an acceptance must (a) be sufficiently communicated to the offeror and (b) mirror the offer in every respect.
    (3)   Consideration is sufficient if it is not so grossly disproportionate as to shock the conscience of the court.

2.   The only possible "given" is consideration. According to *dictum* in the majority opinion in *Derek*, the test is whether the consideration is "so grossly disproportionate that it would shock the conscience of the court to enforce the contract." Under this rule, a selling price of 10% of the value may be sufficiently shocking, and consideration will be an issue. The dissenting judge in *Derek* suggests the rule that "any consideration, no matter how small, is generally sufficient." If the court adopts this rule, consideration will not be an issue. The *dictum* in *Derek* would probably apply because it is from a majority opinion. Thus, consideration is probably an issue and not a "given."

3.   Using the format shown on page 71, the issues and sub-issues look like this:

    (1)   Whether McKay made an effective offer to sell the yacht to Green.
    (2)   Whether Green validly accepted the offer.
        a.   Whether Green sufficiently communicated his acceptance to McKay.
        b.   Whether Green's acceptance mirrored McKay's offer.
    (3)   Whether there was adequate consideration to support the contract (if students conclude consideration is an issue).

Exercise 6-B

The factual and legal materials for this exercise are also used in Exercises 9-B, 11-B, and 12-B.

This is a good problem for introducing students to statutes. The problem also raises some interesting challenges for analysis of elements. The highly charged factual situation on which the problem is based also gives an opportunity to discuss the role of law and lawyering, a discussion that the teacher or the class could develop in several ways.

1.   The initial challenge to this problem is finding the operative statutory language. That language is in sections 3 and 4 because they set out the legal rules on which the newspaper would base a claim for release of the records. It often helps to walk students through these two sections. Section 4 provides the statutory basis for a potential lawsuit

to compel disclosure of the police records. But the newspaper cannot use section 4 unless it has first made a request under section 3(a). Walking students through the wording of section 3(a) shows that the elements include three terms defined in section 2—person, governmental body, and public record. That may lead to a discussion about the relationship between substantive provisions and definitions in a statute. The discussion should also include section 3(b).

Because section 4 provides the basis for a potential suit, its elements are the ones that students must ultimately consider. Of course, many of these elements are also contained in section 3. It is also important to review the possible exemptions under section 5. Note that this leads to two overall questions, which contain the following elements:

(1)   Whether the *Banner-Patriot* meets the statutory requirements for filing a suit.
   a.   Whether the Police Department is a governmental body.
   b.   Whether the Police Department denied a request.
   c.   Whether the *Banner-Patriot* is a "requesting person."
   d.   Whether the police files on the CLO investigation are "public records."
   e.   Whether the *Banner-Patriot* allowed the Police Department five days to respond to its request.

(2)   Whether the Police Department may exempt the records from disclosure.
   a.   Whether the files are (i) records of law enforcement agencies that deal with the detection and investigation of crime, or (ii) internal records and notations of such law enforcement agencies which are maintained for its internal use in matters related to law enforcement.
        If so, whether the files fit this exception (based on *Wheeler* case): "Offense Reports" describing the offense committed, the surrounding circumstances, witnesses, and investigating officers.
   b.   Whether the files contain information of a personal nature where the public disclosure of the information would constitute a clearly unwarranted invasion of an individual's privacy.

It may be helpful to ask whether the exemption rules should, in turn, be divided into elements. That discussion could lead to some interesting questions about how the elements should be understood and analyzed. What, for instance, is the difference between "information of a personal nature" and information the disclosure of which would "constitute a clearly unwarranted invasion of an individual's privacy"? Students might respond that some personal information (habits, appearance, relationships) is well known to others, and some is more private.

2.   No. While this issue may become relevant if the newspaper prints the story, it is not relevant to the question asked: whether the newspaper can obtain the information from the police department.

3.   The Police Department's prompt response complied with section 3(b) of the Act.

4. "Givens":

    (1)   "governmental body." The term includes a "department" of a "county, city, or township." The Star City Police Department is a governmental body.

    (2)   denies a request. The Police Department denied the request.

    (3)   the requesting person. "Person" means an individual, corporation, partnership, firm organization, or association." Both Mickel and the newspaper qualify as persons.

    (4)   "public record." The term includes a "writing prepared, owned, used, in the possession of or retained by a governmental body." The police files are a public record.

    (5)   "waited five business days." The Police Department denied the request in three days.

Thus, the basic prerequisites for filing a suit in sections 3 and 4 have been met.

5. The remaining issues are whether the police records and personal privacy exceptions in sections 5(a) and (d) apply here.

The police records exception may apply because these are records of a law enforcement agency that "deal with the detection and investigation of crime" and are "internal records and notations . . . maintained for its internal use in matters related to law enforcement." However, the *Wheeler Publishing* case indicates that not all records that seem to fall under 5(a) are exempt. It recognizes a right of the public to know certain information about law enforcement efforts in the community and balances this right to know with the police department's need to protect its operations and the individuals involved. That suggests this issue: Is the information in the CLO files "information concerning crime or law enforcement activity in the community," even though no CLO members have ever been arrested for illegal activity associated with their membership? Resolution of this issue will require a determination of whether disclosing the information about the membership, structure, and activities of the CLO would jeopardize the Police Department's law enforcement activities.

The personal privacy exception may apply to at least some of the information in the police records. Although the mayor's wife is the focus of this issue, it is not clear that her involvement is any more "personal" than that of anyone else. Section 5(d) was added to the Act after the *Holcombe* case and is intended at a minimum to protect from disclosure the names of rape victims. Voluntary participation in a racist paramilitary organization seems like a significantly different situation. However, to the extent that these are not law enforcement records, they may include personal information. For example, a court might consider the membership of CLO to be "personal," analogizing the situation to First Amendment freedom-of-association cases. That suggests a second issue: Is the information in the CLO files of a "personal nature," the disclosure of which would constitute a "clearly unwarranted invasion of privacy"?

Additional Exercises[4]

From the examples and exercises in the text, students learned that in order to decide whether a particular element has been satisfied, one must pay attention to whether and how that element has been defined. The exercises below reinforce this idea by requiring students to look at the definition of an element and include that definition in their list of elements.

The burglary issue in Exercise 6-C also illustrates that elements are sometimes interrelated so that whether one is met depends on its relationship to another. On the other hand, Exercise 6-D, a false imprisonment problem, requires students to distinguish between two elements—confinement and consciousness of confinement—that appear to be similar because some of the same facts are relevant to each. They are, however, two distinct elements, as is apparent from the majority and dissenting opinions in *Cay v. City of Greenwood*.

Exercise 6-C

One winter day Jeremy Howe, a homeless person, observed the occupants of a house putting suitcases into their car and driving off. That night, he decided to go inside the house and see if he could find something to eat and a warm place to sleep. All of the doors and windows were locked, but he did find that a door to an unattached garage was unlocked. He pushed the door open and went in. Part of the garage had been converted to an office, with a desk, chair, filing cabinet, and couch. He did not find any food in the garage, so he went to sleep on the couch. The next morning, he searched again for some food, to no avail, but he did find $500 in an envelope in a desk drawer. He took the money and left. A neighbor saw him walking out of the garage and called the police, who arrested him for burglary.

In this state burglary is defined as breaking and entering the dwelling of another with the intent to commit a felony therein. Breaking is the use of force, however slight, in order to gain entry. Entering is the act of going into the dwelling of another without the consent of the occupant. Larceny is the taking and carrying away, with intent to steal, the personal property of another. If the property taken is worth $20 or more, the larceny is a felony; otherwise, it is a misdemeanor.

1.   Make an outline of the elements of burglary.

2.   Indicate which elements have been satisfied in this case and which are likely to be at issue.

---

[4] As noted earlier, Exercise 6-C and Exercise 5-E in this teacher's manual both analyze authorities on burglary. The statutory rule in Exercise 5-E, however, did not require a "breaking," while the common law rule in Exercise 6-C does. If you use both of these examples with your students, we suggest that you remind them that the definitions of many crimes and causes of action differ from state to state. Similarly, Exercise 6-D analyzes a false imprisonment claim. Students will see this cause of action again as an example in Chapter 19 in the text.

The chart below lists the elements and identifies those likely to be at issue.

Elements Chart	
Elements	**Element satisfied?**
Breaking	Maybe
Use of force, however slight,	Yes
In order to gain entry;	Yes
Entering	Maybe
Going into the dwelling of another	Maybe
Without the consent of the occupant;	Yes
Dwelling of another	Maybe
With intent to commit a felony therein.	Probably not

Comments: The elements of breaking, entering, and dwelling of another are interrelated, since they will be satisfied only if the unattached garage is considered a dwelling. If the garage is a dwelling, the breaking element is clearly satisfied because pushing the door open is the use of force, however slight. Breaking and entering are also related to intent. Some students will conclude that this element is satisfied because Howe took $500 with the intent to steal it, which is a felony. However, one must break and enter with the intent to commit a larceny. Howe's intent at the time he broke and entered was to steal some food, which is probably not a felony, and find a warm place to sleep. Therefore, this element is probably not met.

Exercise 6-D

Your client is Juan Velasco, a photographer for a Mexican sports magazine, who was injured while he was filming a tennis match between Jim Davis of the United States and Luis Guerrero of Argentina during the International Tennis Tournament (ITT) held in your city. Guerrero is a very popular player and had a substantial number of vocal supporters in the audience. Davis, who is known for his quick temper, became quite angry early in the match because of the crowd's support of Guerrero and also because of some questionable line calls. He had several arguments with the chair umpire and linesmen, during which the crowd booed. Finally, the chair umpire told Davis to either play tennis or forfeit the match. The next ball that Davis hit went into the net. He swore and threw his racket across the court. The racket ricocheted off a metal post and hit Velasco in the face.

Rhonda Smith was a volunteer recruited by the ITT to work in the first aid tent at the tennis center. She was on duty during the Davis-Guerrero match. After the tennis racquet hit Velasco, an usher escorted him to the first aid tent where Smith applied an antiseptic and adhesive bandage to the facial cuts. She learned from the usher that a volatile situation was developing in the stadium, and she could hear the crowd chanting and yelling. She decided to call the ITT office and ask for advice about what she should do. Because of earlier outbreaks of violence, the volunteers and employees of ITT had been ordered to "take whatever steps are appropriate to avoid incidents and 'bad press.'" She was told to keep Velasco there until a delegation of ITT officials could talk to him.

Smith and Velasco had to communicate by signs and motions because she spoke only English and he spoke only Spanish. After talking to the ITT office, she motioned to Velasco to remain where he was. Several times, he indicated that he would like to use the telephone but

Smith shook her head, indicating "no." When he indicated that he would like to leave, she motioned him back to his chair. During this interval, Velasco was still dazed from the blow he had received. He had a severe headache and was having trouble seeing out of one eye. He knew that he needed medical attention, but he thought that Smith had called a doctor or an ambulance. After almost an hour had elapsed, Velasco decided to leave the tent and try to find an interpreter who could explain to him what was going on. He tried to communicate this desire to Rhonda but again she motioned him to stay. When you asked Velasco why he had not simply left, he replied, "I thought the lady might be a police officer. She was wearing a uniform and seemed to have authority. So when she motioned to me that I should stay, I stayed. I did not want to get into any kind of trouble."

About an hour after Smith called ITT, three officials and an interpreter arrived. The ITT representatives asked Velasco to make a public statement that the incident had been a mere accident and should not be blown out of proportion. They also said that the city did not want any more bad publicity, and they agreed to reimburse Velasco for his medical expenses and lost income if he would make such a statement. Velasco would not agree to make such a statement and demanded that he be taken to a hospital. One of the ITT representatives took Velasco to the emergency room at a hospital, where he was treated for facial lacerations and bleeding in one eye and released.

Your task is to determine whether Velasco has a cause of action for false imprisonment against ITT. You may assume that Smith is an agent for ITT and therefore ITT will be liable if she falsely imprisoned Velasco. You have found the following cases from your state.[5]

Cay v. City of Greenwood (1987)

Appellant Donald Cay appeals from the trial court's dismissal of his claim against the City of Greenwood for false imprisonment. Two police officers employed by the City responded to a call that there was a fight in progress and encountered Donald Cay and several other people engaged in a brawl. Everyone ran away except Cay. The police officers determined that Cay was intoxicated, ordered him into the patrol car, and asked where he lived. Cay told the officers he did not have an address. Rather than taking him to the overnight lock-up facility in the local jail, the officers drove him to a campground outside the city limits where there were shelters and toilet facilities. The campground was not fenced in or otherwise barricaded. The officers claim that this is standard operating procedure when they pick up drunks who are homeless.

Cay has said that he does not remember much about the evening, but he does remember complaining to the officers that they were leaving him "out in the middle of nowhere." During the night, in an apparent attempt to find his way back to Greenwood, Cay wandered onto a highway adjacent to the campground. He was struck by a car and severely injured.

For a cause of action for false imprisonment the plaintiff must show that the defendant intended to confine him, that the plaintiff was conscious of confinement, and that the plaintiff did not consent to the confinement.

[5] The cases are based on *Parvi v. City of Kingston*, 362 N.E.2d 960 (N.Y. 1977), and *Hoffman v. Clinic Hospital, Inc.*, 197 S.E. 161 (N.C. 1938).

It cannot be contended that the police officers, in view of the direct and willful nature of their actions, did not intend to confine Cay. Nor is it arguable that Cay consented. Whether Cay was conscious of confinement in light of his intoxicated state presents a closer question. The trial court concluded that he was not because of his testimony that he had no recollection of his confinement. In so doing, the court failed to distinguish between a later recollection of consciousness and consciousness at the time of confinement. Cay's statement that the officers were leaving him "out in the middle of nowhere" demonstrates some awareness of what was happening to him. It was for the jury to determine whether Cay was indeed aware of his arrest at the time it took place. Reversed.

Baxter, J., dissenting. For a false imprisonment claim, there must be evidence of actual confinement. In this case, there was no confinement, only an exclusion from one area. Once the officers left Cay at the campground, he was unrestrained and free to depart at any time, which he did of his own accord and to his misfortune. I would affirm the trial court's dismissal of the case.

Kaufman v. Central Hospital, Inc. (1948)

Edith Kaufman brought an action against Central Hospital for false imprisonment in the hospital. The trial court entered judgment for the hospital.

Kaufman entered the hospital for treatment and three days later was told by her doctor that she could leave. On that same day, the hospital manager came to her room and told her she could not leave without paying the hospital bill. Kaufman stayed for two more days and then decided to leave, even though she did not have the money to pay her bill. She testified that no one restrained her by any kind of force.

False imprisonment is the restraint of a person against his will by force, or by an express or implied threat of force. Merely considering oneself restrained is not sufficient unless there is a reasonable apprehension that force will be used upon an attempt to assert one's liberty. In this case, the hospital employees employed neither force nor threats of force to restrain Kaufman. She left the hospital without paying her bill and no attempt was made to prevent her from going. Judgment for the hospital was property entered. Affirmed.

1. List the rule(s), and elements of the rule(s), in this problem

2. Are there any elements you would exclude from analysis because they are "givens"? If so, which ones?

3. Identify the issues and sub-issues (if any) in this problem.

The chart below lists the elements of the rule and identifies the issues.

Elements Chart	
Elements	**Element satisfied?**
Intent to confine	Yes
Confinement	Maybe
By the use of force, or	No
By the use of threats, express or implied	Maybe
Consciousness of confinement	Maybe
No consent	Yes

Comments: The closest question is whether Velasco reasonably apprehended a threat to use force if he left. Smith simply motioned him to stay when he tried to leave, but his belief that she might be a police officer and their inability to communicate because of the language barrier might make his apprehension reasonable. The lack of verbal communication, as well as his dazed condition, also raises the issue whether he was conscious of confinement.

Exercise 6-E

Your client is Ann Darnell. Ann's older sister, Sarah Lucas, was a well-know artist before her death a few weeks ago. Sarah and Ann had not been on good terms for a number of years, for reasons that Ann did not want to divulge. On her twenty-first birthday, Ann received a card from Sarah that stated, "My gift is a portrait of you that I have been working on for several months now. I still have a little work to do and then it is yours. Let's let bygones be bygones. Love, Sarah." Ann told you that she did not acknowledge or respond to the card. She still harbored some bitterness toward Sarah, and she told her mother that she did not want to just take the painting and resume an amicable relationship with Sarah before she and Sarah had a chance to sit down and talk about their problems.

Three weeks later, Sarah left town to attend an art show and was fatally injured in an automobile accident. The morning that she left, Sarah sent Ann an e-mail message saying that she had finished the portrait but had not gotten a chance to deliver it before she had to leave town. She told Ann that it was in her studio and that Ann could get a key from their mother and take the painting home with her. Ann did not read the message until after she heard that Sarah had been killed. When she went to the studio several days later, she discovered that it was empty. Sarah's husband had removed all the paintings. He is claiming that the portrait belongs to him because in her will Sarah left him all of her personal property except for some furniture and jewelry that she left to friends and other members of her family. Ann now regrets that she was so unforgiving and did not welcome Sarah's overture to settle the discord between them. She would like to have the portrait that she claims Sarah gave her. The issue in this case is whether there was a valid gift inter vivos. You have found three cases from your state:[6]

---

[6] The three cases are based on *In re Will of Gorden,* 27 N.W.2d 900 (Iowa 1947); *In re Marriage of Elam*, No. 3-971/03-0221, 2004 Iowa App. LEXIS 308 (Feb. 27 2004); and *Gray v. Roth*, 438 N.W.2d 25 (Iowa Ct. App. 1989).

In re Will of Bratton (1947)

Martha Bratton died in 1944. In her will, she left her estate to her nephew, James Abbott, and her sister, Lucille Nichols. Previously, Martha had sent James $5,000 along with a letter instructing him that at her death, he was to divide the money equally among himself, his brother, and his two sisters. The executor of Martha's estate filed a petition with the court, asking that the $5,000 be adjudicated as part of the deceased's estate. The trial denied the petition and the executor appeals. We affirm.

The money that Martha entrusted to James was a valid gift *inter vivos*. A gift *inter vivos*, by definition, must be completed during the lifetime of the donor. Martha's letter showed her clear intent to make such a gift. By giving the money to James with instructions to hold it for the donees, Martha relinquished all right to and dominion over the money. Direct delivery to the donees is not required; it may be made to a person acting as agent or trustee for the donees. If the gift is complete, it will not be defeated by postponement of the enjoyment of the gift until the death of the donor.

Nielson v. Keating, Executor (2002)

Lucy Nielsen appeals from a decision by the trial court that certain bonds were the jointly owned property of Lucy and her ex-husband Frank Nielsen, now deceased. The Nielsens were recently divorced. Shortly after the divorce, Frank was killed in a boating accident. In the dissolution of marriage proceeding, the court concluded that the bonds were co-owned by husband and wife and therefore marital property. Lucy appeals, claiming that the bonds were an inter vivos gift to her.

The decedent owned the bonds at the time of his marriage to Lucy. After the marriage, he had the bonds reissued in his name and Lucy's name. State Code § 235.2 provides that in a dissolution of marriage proceeding, the court "shall divide all property, except inherited property or gifts received by one party, equitably between the parties."

The trial court correctly held that there was no valid gift of the bonds from the decedent to Lucy. A gift requires donative intent and delivery. The donor must relinquish title, dominion, and control of the gift. By leaving his name on the bonds as co-owner, decedent retained control of the bonds and could have cashed them at any time. Affirmed.

In re Marriage of Judson (2004)

Lucretia Judson appeals from a provision of the divorce decree dissolving her marriage to Edwin Judson. In the contested provision, the court granted Edwin title to an airplane that Lucretia purchased with her separate funds while she was married to Edwin. The court concluded that the airplane was a gift from Lucretia to Edwin, based on the following evidence: Lucretia had title to the airplane, but she was not a licensed pilot and never flew the plane. Edwin, who is a licensed pilot, flew the plane regularly and took charge of maintenance, repairs, and payment of fees and taxes. Lucretia had also given Edwin a framed picture of the airplane with the caption "Edwin's Private Airplane," which hung on the wall in his office. State Code § 235.2 provides that in a dissolution of marriage proceeding the court shall divide all property "except inherited property or gifts received by one party."

The requirements of a valid gift are: donative intent, delivery, and acceptance. Acceptance is usually presumed if the gift is beneficial, unless there is evidence to the contrary. Intent is the controlling element, but delivery must be as complete as the circumstances allow. Because Lucretia gave Edwin control of and free access to the airplane and denominated it "Edwin's Private Plane, " thus fulfilling the elements of intent and delivery, we find no error in the trial court's decision that the plane was a gift . Affirmed.

1. List the rule(s), and elements of the rule(s), in this problem.

2. Are there any elements you would exclude from analysis because they are "givens"? If so, which ones?

3. Identify the issues and sub-issues (if any) in the problem.

The chart below identifies the elements, issues, and sub-issues.

Elements Chart	
Elements of a gift inter vivos	*Element satisfied?*
Intent to make a gift	Yes
Delivery	Maybe
Relinquishment of dominion and control	Maybe
As complete as circumstances allow	Maybe
Acceptance	Maybe
During the lifetime of the donor	Maybe

Comments: By leaving a message that Ann could get the key to her studio and take the portrait, Sarah arguably relinquished dominion and control and made a delivery as complete as the circumstances allow. Ann probably did not accept until after the death of the donor, but a court could presume prior acceptance because she did not explicitly reject the gift and it is beneficial to her.

7
Common Law Analysis

Changes From the Second Edition

There are no major changes or significant minor changes from the second edition.

Teaching Notes

Some teachers find it helpful to teach this chapter in conjunction with Chapter 9 (Reaching a Conclusion). One of the authors works with students to combine the elements charts demonstrated in Chapter 6 (Identifying & Selecting Issues for Analysis) with the analysis charts demonstrated in Chapters 7 (Common Law Analysis) and 8 (Statutory Analysis) into a single "elements and analysis chart." Developing such a chart can be a very effective pre-writing technique, and it is easier for some students to start with the familiar chart format rather than with a traditional outline. A sample "elements and analysis" chart based on the shopkeeper's privilege statute and cases in Exercises 5-F and 5-G appears in Appendix F of this manual.

Suggested Approach to Exercises

Exercise 7-A

This exercise may work better in class (without prior announcement) than as a writing assignment because Chapter 14 (Drafting the Discussion) uses both of the libel sub-issues from this chapter to teach drafting of the Discussion. Students are less likely to peek ahead to Chapter 14 for clues when you use the exercise this way. On the other hand, using this exercise means that the class will better understand the analysis of this sub-issue when they reach Chapter 14.

The analysis shown here does not contain charts, although you can easily develop them.

1.   Determine how the facts of the decided cases support your client's position. It is often helpful to remind students that they must start their analysis of the usefulness of cases by understanding the holdings. Both *Willow* and *White* held that the allegedly libelous statements were substantially accurate. That is the holding Dooley wants. Thus, the student's job is to develop explanations of how these cases are analogous to Dooley's situation. The fact patterns in the two cases are similar enough to let a teacher begin to talk about synthesizing, or analyzing several cases at the same time. You could thus ask students to apply each case separately to Dooley's situation, and then analogize them together. The best answers will explain why the statement that Fremont has "a long record of criminal violations" is substantially the same as a statement that he had three notices of violation for housing code violations and had to be threatened to correct them. To say that someone is criminal, students sometimes argue, is to say that the person has done bad things, and does not necessarily mean that the person has been convicted of a crime.

2. Determine how the facts of the decided cases support your opponent's position. Students will generally find it easier to make distinctions. One approach is to ask students to explain the differences between each case and Dooley's situation, and then explain how the two cases taken together are different from Dooley's situation. This type of work again anticipates the synthesis lesson in Chapter 11 (Describing the Law). Students generally make these arguments by showing that the statement in the fliers is much less accurate than the statements in *Willow* and *White*.

3. Determine how the reasons and policies of the decided cases support your client's position. The Willow court reasoned that legal terms like kidnapping should be analyzed as they would be ordinarily understood rather than as they would be understood in a technical legal context. Similarly, Dooley might argue, the statement about Fremont's criminal record as a landlord would be understood, by ordinary people, as meaning only that Fremont was an irresponsible landlord. The implicit policy in *White* is the court's unwillingness to impose libel liability on persons for minor inaccuracies. The inaccuracy in this case, your client may argue, is similarly minor.

4. Determine how the reasons and policies of the decided cases support your opponent's position. Your opponent would emphasize the other side of the same policies. If someone is substantially wrong, your opponent would argue, he should be held liable for libel. The gist of the matter is that Dooley's statement was false. As the White court noted, receipt of false statements by third persons is what makes libel so damaging.

5. Evaluate the strength of your client's case. Using the Chapter 8 factors for reaching a conclusion, the evaluation looks like this in summary form:

➤ A decision that the statements are false involves the least extension of existing law. The "long record of criminal convictions" language would make it difficult for a court to hold that Dooley's statement was mere hyperbole.

➤ A decision that the statements are false is most consistent with the basic purpose of the libel law—protection of a person's reputation.

➤ The fairness issue in this case is more of a toss-up because each party can make compelling arguments (it was an accident vs. it hurt my reputation).

We would conclude that the statements are false.

Exercise 7-B

The factual and legal materials for this exercise are also used in Exercises 14-B(1) and 24-B.

1. A doctor is liable if (1) his negligent diagnosis or treatment (2) prevents a substantial possibility of recovery or survival.

2. Yes. Both cases are binding precedent.

3./4. These questions can be answered in greater detail, but at a minimum these points should be covered:

The *Moulton* decision offers some support for Quale. Like the patient in *Moulton*, Andrew died because a doctor failed to diagnose his condition. The *Moulton* court reasoned that a doctor would be liable if the patient would have survived if the doctor's diagnosis and treatment had not been negligent. Quale must argue that Andrew's "1 chance out of 3" of surviving was a "substantial possibility" and within the rule adopted in *Moulton*. The underlying policy in *Moulton* is helpful because it states that the plaintiff need not show certainty to recover.

The *Mallard* decision offers some support for Farmer. The court in *Mallard* held that the doctor's negligent diagnosis and failure to treat his patient did not proximately cause the patient's paralysis because the patient had only a "possibility" of recovery and "probably would not have recovered" even with proper diagnosis and treatment. Andrew Quale's situation was similar. He had only a 50/50 chance, 1 chance out of 2, of surviving even if the doctor had not been negligent. The policy announced by the *Mallard* court also supports Farmer. As a matter of public policy, a doctor should not be "held accountable for harm that he did not cause and may not have been able to prevent."

Quale, however, can attempt to distinguish *Mallard*. Unlike the patient in *Mallard* who "probably would not have recovered," Andrew had a 50/50 chance of survival, "maybe a little higher." Quale might argue that it was therefore "more likely than not" that Andrew would have survived had Farmer not been negligent.

5. This is an extremely close case, but Farmer is most likely to prevail. The cases are based on a "more likely than not" standard, which is the traditional common law causation standard. A court is likely to find that a 1 in 2 chance does not quite meet that standard. The *Mallard* case supports that conclusion. The *Moulton* case, which Quale must rely on, is distinguishable because the patient in *Moulton* would definitely have recovered. The substantial-possibility language in *Moulton* suggests a weaker standard, but the *Mallard* court uses "substantial possibility" and "more likely than not" interchangeably. Students will reach different conclusions, however, depending on the weight they give to Quale's expert's opinion that Andrew's chance of survival might have been "a little higher" than 50/50.

The policies underlying the cases—not holding a doctor liable based on a mere possibility, and not requiring plaintiffs to show causation with certainty—probably tip in favor of Farmer. The "more likely than not" standard is consistent with both policies.

Fairness is a toss-up here. The doctor was negligent, but it is not clear whether the boy probably would <u>not</u> have survived or had a slightly better than 50/50 chance of survival. Although this factor is closer, the first two tip the balance slightly toward Farmer.

Exercise 7-C

The factual and legal materials for this exercise are also used in Exercises 14-B(2) and 25-B.

1. Suggest to students that in order to identify the issues, they should begin by listing the applicable rules and dividing the rules into component elements.

►   The rule from *Shover* is that a property owner is liable if he (1) injures (2) the legal rights of another property owner.

►   The rule from *Horton* is that a property owner is liable if he (1) interferes with the peaceful enjoyment of property by another and (2) the interference is unreasonable.

►   The rule from *Blum* is the same. Reasonableness is measured by the effect of one property owner's activity on the neighboring property.

►   The rule from *Cassells* is the same as *Shover*. It found no legal right to the free flow of sunlight.

A synthesized rule incorporating each element would look like this: A property owner is liable for nuisance if (a) the owner interferes with (b) the legal rights of another property owner *and* (c) the other owner suffers injury *and* (d) the interference is unreasonable. These rules give rise to two "givens" (one owner's interference and the other owner's injury) and two issues:

(1) Does Greenleaf have a legal right to the free flow of sunlight?
(2) If so, did Elliot unreasonably interfere with that right?

2./ 3. Outline the case support for each issue separately.

Issue (1)

<u>Rule</u>: Landowners must enjoy their property so as not to injure legal rights in the property of another. *Shover*

<u>Issue</u>: Does Greenleaf have a legal right to the free flow of sunlight?

Case support for Greenleaf

The rule in *Shover* is broad enough to include the right to the free flow of light. The rule in *Cassells* that there is no right to the free flow of light is not binding and should not be followed. The rule was formulated before society's interest in encouraging the development of alternative energy sources. Reasons for the rule are not as strong today.

The damage to Greenleaf is much greater than the damage suffered in *Cassells*. There, the hotel owner anticipated potential economic loss and inconvenience to its guests. Here, Greenleaf's business might be destroyed because potential customers can see that solar energy will not work if neighbors can block the sunlight. Even if Greenleaf's business survives, the potential damage is similar to that in *Shover*, where the loss of lateral support "greatly devalued" the property.

Case support for Elliot

The rule in *Cassells* is the traditional common law rule. No American court has ever recognized a right to the free flow of light. *Shover* is inapplicable because it concerned the right to lateral support.

The reasons for the rule are just as valid today. Requiring that every property owner allow the free flow of sunlight onto neighboring property would make building construction in high-density areas economically unfeasible and would infringe on individual property rights.

Cassells is analogous because the damages to Greenleaf and to the hotel owner are similar. Both suffered some economic damage and some inconvenience in carrying on their respective businesses.

Issue (2)

Rule: A property owner is liable if he unreasonably interferes with another owner's peaceful enjoyment of his property. *Horton*

Issue: Did Elliot unreasonably interfere with Greenleaf's enjoyment of Greenleaf's property by erecting billboards that block the sun from the solar panels on the office building Greenleaf uses to promote the use of solar energy?

Case support for Greenleaf

Just as the landfill owner's trucks in *Blum* essentially destroyed the neighboring hog farmer's business by causing the sows' conception rate to decrease from 80% to 30%, so the billboards are essentially destroying Greenleaf's business by making his promotional appeal less attractive and increasing his cost of doing business substantially. Such a practice amounts to confiscation and is *per se* unreasonable. *Blum*

The *Horton* court upheld damages against a landowner who dusted his crops with a spray that was toxic to a neighboring farmer's bees because the spraying was an unreasonable interference with the neighbor's use of his property as a melon farm. Elliot's interference with Greenleaf's solar energy business is at least as unreasonable.

Case support for Elliot

The court will balance the interests of each landowner. *Blum*. In *Horton* the crop duster could have easily prevented the damage by spraying on a calm day. Elliot, however, cannot prevent the damage to Greenleaf without substantial cost.

It is unreasonable to ask Elliot to remove his property and risk losing substantial business. The interference with Greenleaf's solar panels is an inconvenience, but it is not a destruction of his business, as was the case in *Blum*.

4.   The rule in *Cassells* would defeat Greenleaf's argument as to Issue (1). It is important that it is from another state because the court in this case is not bound by it. Greenleaf can thus argue that the trial court should reject the *Cassells* rule.

5.   Greenleaf's position as to Issue (1) is weak because the common law rule, according to *Cassells*, is that there is no right to the free flow of sunlight. He would have to convince the court to reject an existing widely recognized rule and formulate a new one. His public policy argument that the courts should promote the use of alternative energy sources is not likely to overcome his weak legal position. Many of our students, on the other hand, believe Greenleaf's position is amply justified and want him to prevail. Although some of us believe Greenleaf ought to prevail, we use this part of the exercise to emphasize the importance of dispassionate analysis.

Greenleaf's position as to Issue (2) is probably stronger than Elliot's. In balancing the interests of the landowners, the scales tip in Greenleaf's favor because his entire business is at stake. The court may also consider that Greenleaf's solar energy promotion has more social utility than Elliot's billboards.

After class discussion of this exercise, you may wish to hand out the annotated sample discussion in Appendix B of this manual. It illustrates how to combine the answers to the questions into an organized discussion.

Additional Exercise

This exercise focuses on factual analogy and distinction and further illustrates the importance of the policies underlying the rule.

One approach to the first issue, whether the pond is a natural or artificial condition, is to explain the close connection between the reason for the rule and the facts. The reason courts impose no duty of reasonable care for natural conditions is that children are presumed to understand the dangers they pose. The question then becomes whether the alterations to the Mayfields' pond so changed its characteristics that children would not appreciate the danger because it was no longer natural.

Another approach is to discuss the difficulty of specifically defining the scope of the term "natural condition." How many and what kind of alternations are necessary before a body of water becomes artificial? Similarly, the second issue hinges on the scope of the duty. What precautions must a landowner take in order to protect trespassing children? These questions cannot be definitively answered. The only reasonable approach is to ascertain the parameters set by the courts in prior cases and consider whether the facts of your case fit within those parameters.

Exercise 7-D

Paul and Judy Mayfield own a house and two-acre lot adjacent to an elementary school. When they bought the property, it contained a small pond, used by the previous owners as a watering hole for cattle. They turned it into an ornamental pond by excavating the sides to create a gradual slope, planting various species of water lilies, and stocking it with goldfish. They installed a recirculating pump and built a dock that runs from the edge of the pond to the center. The pond is roughly circular and about forty feet in diameter. It is six feet deep at the center and tapers to a depth of about eight inches at the edges. Paul and Judy use the dock for sunbathing, entertaining guests, and servicing the pump when necessary. After the renovation of the pond was completed, they installed a four-foot-high cedar picket fence around the one-half acre in the backyard where the pond is located.

Earlier this year, several children from the elementary school, including Alan Finch, climbed over the fence, went down to the pond, and walked out onto the dock to watch the goldfish. Judy Mayfield told the children to leave her property and stay away from the pond. After that incident, she put up a sign along the fence that read "DO NOT CLIMB FENCE." Several weeks later, on a day when the Mayfields were not at home, Alan Finch and two friends decided to visit the pond again. Alan had some goldfish food and wanted to feed the fish. At one end of the yard, they found a gate standing slightly ajar, entered through the gate, and went down to the pond. The gate through which they entered is the only gate. It has a latch but no lock. Alan went to the end of the dock, slipped, and fell into the pond. Since Alan could not swim, his friends jumped in and attempted a rescue. After several minutes, they succeeded in pulling him onto the dock. Alan survived but suffered brain damage because of the deprivation of oxygen to his brain.

Alan's parents, Joseph and Carol Finch, have asked you whether the Mayfields are liable for Alan's injuries. You have found the following cases from your state: [7]

Vernon v. Earnhart (1984)

This wrongful death action arose out of the drowning of five-year-old Leroy Vernon in a pond located on the property of Max and Sarah Earnhart. James and Rosalyn Vernon, who live next door to the Earnharts, were outside working in their garden when they noticed that Leroy was missing. One of their other children said that Leroy had gone next door to look at the ducks on the Earnharts' pond. The Vernons rushed over to the pond but were too late to save Leroy. He had apparently waded into the pond, lost his footing, and drowned. The Vernons maintain that the pond is an attractive nuisance and that the Earnharts were negligent in failing to anticipate and guard against the danger it presented to

---

[7] The cases are drawn from *Johnson v. Washington County*, 506 N.W.2d 632 (Minn. Ct. App. 1993), *aff'd.*, 518 N.W.2d 594 (Minn. 1994); *Adams v. Atlantic Faith Memorial Church,, Inc.*, 381 S.E.2d 397 (Ga. Ct. App. 1989); *Gregory v. Johnson*, 289 S.E.2d 232 (Ga. 1982); and *Watts v. Murray*, 43 So. 2d 303 (La. Ct. App. 1949).

children. The trial court dismissed the Vernons' suit against the Earnharts for failure to state a cause of action. We affirm.

A possessor of land is liable for injuries to children trespassing on the land only if the injuries were caused by an artificial condition on the land and the possessor failed to use reasonable care to eliminate the danger or otherwise protect the children. A possessor of land is not liable for natural conditions on the land. This distinction between artificial and natural conditions is based on the premise that children are presumed to appreciate the danger of conditions which occur in nature.

We agree with the trial court that the pond, which was constructed by the Vernons for the purposes of swimming and boating, is not an artificial condition. Changes in natural environments do not create an artificial condition where the affected terrain duplicates nature. The pond is seven feet deep at the center and has a sandy beach and a sloping sandy bottom. The only artificial characteristic is the cement walkway. We cannot characterize the entire pond as artificial based on such a minimal change in its natural condition.

Ward v. Kirlin (1992)

Steve and Grace Kirlin appeal from a decision by the trial court finding them liable for the death of a four-year-old child who wandered onto their property from the neighboring property and drowned in their swimming pool. The child's parent, Sally Ward, brought an action in negligence against the Kirlins for maintaining an attractive nuisance. The issue on appeal is whether the Kirlins owed a duty to the trespassing child to protect him from the danger posed by the swimming pool and if so, whether there was sufficient evidence that they breached that duty.

The Kirlins' house is on a corner lot in a residential area. The pool is in the side yard, visible from the street, and is equipped with a diving board and slide. The Kirlins had failed to erect a fence or other barriers around the pool, even though they had been warned that the presence of the pool and its playground-like equipment was likely to attract children.

The rule, long observed in this state, is that the attractive nuisance doctrine does not apply to bodies of water such as rivers and streams. Requiring landowners to alter land in its natural state for the benefit of trespassers would place an unacceptable burden on them. The rule, however, has not been considered in the context of a swimming pool. We hold that the attractive nuisance doctrine does apply to landowners who maintains a swimming pool on their property and that they have a duty to exercise reasonable care to guard against harm to trespassing children who cannot appreciate the danger posed by the artificial condition. There is no doubt that the deceased child in this case was a trespasser, since he came upon the property uninvited, and that he was too young to appreciate the danger. The failure of the Kirlins to take any steps, such as building a fence, to protect children who might foreseeably come upon their property amounts to a breach of the duty of reasonable care. Affirmed.

Saylor v. Renfro Art Museum **(1999)**

The trial court awarded summary judgment to Renfro Art Museum in a negligence claim filed against it by Phillip Saylor, whose six-year-old son drowned in a small ornamental pool located in a fenced, wooded area owned by the museum and adjacent to the apartment complex where the Saylors live. Saylor appeals, claiming that the museum maintained an attractive nuisance and failed to exercise reasonable care to eliminate the danger to children posed by the pool. The pool is located in a formal garden underneath a fountain. It is made of concrete and is approximately four feet deep and eight feet in diameter. The pool and garden are hidden by woods. A chain link fence surrounds the museum property and another chain link fence surrounds the garden. The Saylor child entered the museum property without permission. While wading in the pool, he apparently slipped, hit his head on the concrete, and drowned

      We find Saylor's claim that the museum failed to exercise reasonable care to be without merit. By erecting two fences, it did all that could reasonably be expected to prevent unauthorized entry. Despite the tragic nature of this occurrence, we cannot place upon a landowner the burden of taking precautions against every conceivable danger to a child who ventures uninvited onto the property. Affirmed.

1.   Identify the rule(s) and elements of the rule(s) in this problem.
2.   For each issue, how do the facts support the Finches' case? the Mayfields' case?
3.   For each issue, how do the reasons and policies of the cases support the Finches' case? the Mayfields' case?
4.   Evaluate the strength of the Finches' position on each issue.

Suggested Approach to Exercise 7-D

1.   A landowner is liable for injury to (1) trespassing children (2) if the injury is caused by an artificial condition on the land, and (3) the landowner failed to use reasonable care to eliminate the danger or protect the children. Element (1) is given. Elements (2) and (3) are issues.

2/3.   <u>Issue 1</u>: Is the ornamental pond a natural condition on the land?

<u>Case support for the Finches</u>

     Vernon is distinguishable. In that case, the cement walkway was the only artificial addition to a pond that duplicated nature. The Mayfields' pond has a dock, a recirculating pump, water lilies, and goldfish. Taken as a whole, these additions changed the pond from its natural state.

     The purpose of the attractive nuisance doctrine is to protect children. *Vernon*. The pond, like the swimming pool in *Ward* with its "playground-like equipment," is attractive to children because of the goldfish and water lilies, whereas an ordinary, unaltered pond would not be. Therefore, children are unlikely to appreciate the danger.

Case support for the Mayfields

Like the pond in *Vernon*, the Mayfields' pond is a natural condition on the land. In *Vernon*, the pond, even though constructed by the landowners, duplicated nature and thus was not an artificial condition. The Mayfields' pond was not even constructed by them, merely reconfigured, and the additions to the pond, such as fish and water lilies, are things commonly found in ponds and do not change its nature. Also, the dock and pump, like the cement walkway in *Vernon*, should be considered minimal changes.

Issue 2: Did the Mayfields exercise reasonable care to eliminate the danger and protect the children?

Case support for the Finches

This case is similar to *Ward*, where the court found a breach of the duty of reasonable care when the landowners failed to erect a fence around their swimming pool. A fence with an open gate is similar to no fence at all because the children had free access to the yard where the pond was located. Although Judy Mayfield had warned the children to stay away, she did not prevent their re-entry. The sign she erected did not forbid entering through the gate, merely climbing the fence. *Saylor* is distinguishable because in that case the owner installed two fences with no openings in them, and the pool was hidden from view by trees, not visible to passing children like the Mayfields' pond.

Case support for the Mayfields

The court in *Ward* implied that a fence is all that is necessary, and the court in *Saylor* found that the owners exercised reasonable care by erecting fences. The Mayfields not only erected a fence but also warned the children to stay away. After they had climbed the fence previously, Judy Mayfield put up a sign saying "Do Not Climb Fence." A landowner is not required to take "precautions against every conceivable danger to a child who ventures uninvited onto the property." *Saylor*.

4. The Mayfields are likely to prevail on the first issue. Although they altered the natural appearance of the pond more than did the owners in *Ward*, the changes are probably not enough for a court to consider the pond artificial.

    The Finches' position as to the second issue is slightly stronger because of the open gate. The *Saylor* case is strong support for the Mayfields, however. They had taken the precautions of warning the children to stay away and not to climb the fence and were not expected to guard against every eventuality.

8
Statutory Analysis

Changes From the Second Edition

There are no major changes and no significant minor changes from the second edition.

Teaching Notes

As with Chapter 7, some teachers find it helpful to use this chapter in conjunction with Chapter 9 (Reaching a Conclusion). Others encourage students to use elements charts and statutory analysis charts together as a pre-writing technique. The example in Appendix F of this manual shows a chart built on a statutory rule as interpreted by two cases.

Consider taking your class to the library to find the rules of statutory construction for the state in which you are located. Some of us also hand out a summary of the principles explained in this chapter, such as the outline below, or distribute a handout that describes some of the most common canons of statutory construction.

Selected Rules of Statutory Construction

Legislative intent. Giving effect to legislative intent is the primary goal in statutory construction and is "trumps" over every other rule. Courts use the following rules and presumptions in trying to ascertain legislative intent.

1. Plain meaning. If the meaning of the statute is plain, the courts' task is to apply it as written. They will not stretch the meaning of a word, phrase, or definition beyond its ordinary meaning. To do so would be judicial legislation.

2. Ambiguity. If the statute is ambiguous, courts will interpret it according their understanding of the purpose of the legislation. They will also make certain presumptions, also known as rules of construction. For example:

    a. Courts will presume that the legislature was aware of existing statutory and common law on the same subject and will interpret the statute in light of prior law.

    b. Courts will presume that the drafters understood the commonly accepted rules of grammar and punctuation and will interpret the statute according to those rules.

    c. Under the rule of *ejusdem generis*, courts will presume that a general term following a specific list of items refers to the same type of items as those in the list.

d.   Courts will presume that the legislature did not intend an unjust or absurd result.

You might also point out that courts use the same general principles in interpreting constitutional provisions. They will strive to give effect to the intent of the drafters and will first look at the plain language of the provision in question. Courts will interpret amendments so as to harmonize them with existing provisions and existing common law, if possible, and will not construe a provision so as to render it purposeless or in conflict with other provisions. However, punctuation, grammar, and sentence structure do not play as large a role in constitutional interpretation as they do in statutory interpretation.

Suggested Approach to Exercises

Exercise 8-A

The factual and legal materials for this exercise are also used in Exercise 13-C(1).

As the elements chart on page 95 indicates, a public body exists when (1) there is a state or local legislative body (2) that is empowered by law to exercise governmental or proprietary functions. The first element focuses on what that body is and the second focuses on what that body does. Thus, the discussion in the text for the second element focuses on whether the four Conservative members could exercise governmental functions based on their majority status even if they do not constitute a quorum. The discussion under the first sub-issue must focus on whether they can be understood to constitute the council or a committee of the council. An outline of the analysis might look like this:

1. Determine how the language of the statute, and the facts of any cases interpreting the statute, support your client's position. The statutory language is in Section 2(b), and there are no cases interpreting that language. The statute applies to "any state or local legislative body, including a board, commission, committee, subcommittee, authority, or council." Because the statute applies to the City Council, your client would want to argue, it surely applies to the majority of the Council. In the alternative, your client might want to argue that the four Conservatives constitute an informal committee of the Council.

2. Determine how the language of the statute, and the facts of any cases interpreting the statute, support your opponent's position. Your opponent would want to argue that section 2(b) applies to the entire council, which must be represented by at least a quorum of its members, or a committee of the Council. Because they do not comprise a quorum or a formal committee, they are not a legislative body. Your opponent would add that the *McPhee* case involved meetings attended by an entire board of education.

3. Determine how the policies of the statute, and the policies of any cases interpreting the statute, support your client's position. Your client's policy arguments would be similar, in part, to those under the governmental functions sub-issue. Meetings of a working majority are intended to accomplish "public business" and would probably have that effect. In some ways, your client's most effective position may be based on the purposes of the committee language. The statute's inclusion of committees in its definition of public bodies recognizes that parts of a council may have a profound impact on public business. If committee meetings must be made public, and committees may not even include enough members to constitute a majority of the council, then surely the meeting of the four Conservatives should be made public. Besides, they constitute a *de facto* budget committee when they decide to operate in this way. Your client would also want to focus on the *McPhee* rationale concerning the importance of opening preliminary meetings to the public.

4. Determine how the policies of the statute, and the policies of any cases interpreting the statute, support your opponent's position. Your opponent's arguments would also parallel those made under the governmental functions sub-issue. The statute recognizes the importance of informal meetings among council members. That is why it applies only to the entire council or formal committees. It makes no sense to say that a legislative body exists without a quorum. Committees ordinarily exist when the council itself appoints them, and they are ordinarily bipartisan. A party caucus is different; there is no committee when the members of one party meet to discuss their position, regardless of whether they constitute a majority.

5. Evaluate the strength of your client's position. The Chapter 9 analysis looks something like this:

► Little or no extension of the law. Your opponent probably has a slight edge here because the four members do not comprise a quorum or a formal committee.

► Purposes of the law. Your client probably has an edge here because the statute is intended to reach committee behavior and because this group is acting like a committee.

► Fairness to the parties. Your client's position is that the Conservative caucus wants to exclude him from discussion that he was elected to participate in. Your opponent would argue that political parties cannot do business if their meetings must be public. Your client would respond that this isn't just a party meeting; it is more like a committee meeting because it is intended to develop a specific position on the budget. Your client probably has an edge here too.

As a result, your client is more likely than not to prevail on this sub-issue.

Exercise 8-B

The strongest argument for the motel owner is based on the plain meaning rule. Because the statute is clear on its face, there is no need to use a rule of construction such as *ejusdem generis* to ascertain its meaning. The ninety-day statute of limitations applies to recovery of "personal property . . . left at a hotel or other public lodging." The car and trailer fit within this category. They are personal property and they were left at a motel.

An alternative argument is that even if the language is ambiguous, it should be read to include vehicles because a traveler is likely to have a vehicle with him when he stays at a motel. The statute doesn't limit the category to property brought into a room. It includes any personal property left "at" a public lodging. This interpretation comports with the implicit intent of the statute—to limit liability to a period of time within which the traveler discovered or could reasonably have discovered that his property was missing.

The second argument is considerably weaker than the first. If the court rejects the plain meaning argument and engages in statutory construction, it is likely to find the construction described above somewhat less credible than the construction applying the *ejusdem generis* rule described on page 99 of the text.

Exercise 8-C

1.   The phrase "such action as will effectuate the purpose of the Act, including, but not limited to" is quite general, and reasonable minds could construe it differently. The broadest construction is that it includes any remedy that furthers the purpose of the Act, which is to eliminate employment discrimination. The narrowest construction is that it is limited to putting the employee in the same employment situation he or she would have been in but for the discrimination.

2.   The *ejusdem generis* rule would apply here, and Jade Enterprises should argue for its application. The remedies listed in section 6 are those that would restore employment benefits the employee lost because of discrimination. Under *ejusdem generis*, the Commission would be authorized to order the employer to provide only those remedies of the same kind or class. It would not be authorized to order the employer to provide other kinds of remedies such as compensatory damages for emotional distress.

Apart from *ejusdem generis*, Jade would argue that the legislature is presumed to be aware of the common law, including existing common law remedies. If the legislature intended to replace or supplement these remedies, it would have said so.

The Commission could invoke the plain meaning rule. Section 6 authorizes it to order actions "including, but not limited to" those that are listed. The Commission would argue that this statutory language expressly defeats the *ejusdem generis* presumption. This language gives the Commission the express authority to fashion other remedies.

A court is likely to presume that the legislature did not intend an unjust result. The Commission could use this presumption to argue that it would be unjust in this situation to award no compensation in light of the judge's finding that Jade had engaged in sexual harassment. The theory is that the legislature did not contemplate situations in which the victim has no remedy except for compensatory damages; if it had, it would have provided such a remedy.

In a real situation, both parties would research common law construing this and similar statutes to see whether they could base an argument on the judicial presumption described on page 99 of the text that the legislature was aware of relevant common law and prior statutes when it enacted the current statute.

Both sides will also argue that legislative intent supports their respective positions. (See answer 3.)

3. The stated purpose of the Act, "to eliminate discrimination .by providing effective remedies" to victims of discrimination, supports the Commission's position because a remedy is effective only if it discourages the employer from practicing discrimination. Unless Jade pays compensatory damages to Preston it will pay nothing. Preston was a temporary employee who worked for the full term of her employment. She lost no wages or other employee benefits and she is not entitled to reinstatement. Allowing Jade to practice sexual harassment without consequence defeats the purpose of the Act.

The Act is also remedial in nature. One of its purposes is to compensate the victim. The only way to compensate Preston in this case is to allow compensatory damages.

4. Jade's position is that the purpose of the Act is to restore to the victim any employment-related compensation and benefits of which she was deprived because of discrimination. In other words, the statutory purpose is to put her in the same position she was in before the illegal acts occurred. In this case, Preston has suffered no loss of pay or benefits. She is already in the same position she was in before. Although another purpose is to discourage discrimination, the legislature did not intend to accomplish this purpose by requiring the employer to pay to the victim anything other than what the victim has lost. Otherwise, it would have given the Commission specific authority to award compensatory, and perhaps even punitive, damages.

5. Although both sides have strong legal and policy arguments, Jade's position is stronger. The primary concern of the court will be to give effect to legislative intent. To find for the Commission, the court would have to read the statutory language more broadly than the legislature probably intended.

Exercise 8-D

The factual and legal materials for this exercise are also used in Exercises 14-C(2) and 24-C. When using this problem, make sure that the students are looking carefully at the wording of the statute and are considering how the case law has interpreted or modified the statute.

1. The applicable rule is State Court Rule 779.1(3) as the court in Halsey has interpreted it. A person "shall be allowed to intervene" in a lawsuit when three elements are met:

    (1)   the application must be "timely";
    (2)   the applicant's interest is or "may be" inadequately represented;
    (3)   the applicant will be "bound" by a judgment, which has been defined by the court as having an interest that will be "substantially affected" by a decision in the case.

2. The Drafting Committee's comment is not binding authority. However, it may persuade the court that the statute was or was not intended to cover the League's situation. The *Halsey* case is binding authority and will be followed by courts in subsequent decisions interpreting the statute.

3.   The League will argue that the language of the statute supports its position:

   ►   The application would be "timely" because it would be filed as soon as the city indicated that the League's interest would no longer be represented in the lawsuit.

   ►   As an organization representing welfare recipients, the League has an interest in the development of low income housing. The League's interest is no longer adequately represented in the action because the city attorney and mayor have now indicated that the city may no longer be supporting the low income housing plan.

   ►   It is hard to argue that the League will be "bound" as that word is used in the dictionary. The League would have to argue that it could not challenge an adverse court decision and that it would be harmed by such a decision.

   The *Halsey* case makes it much easier for the League to meet the third element. The court says a party is "bound" when, "as a practical matter," its ability to protect its interests "may be substantially affected." Like the property owners in *Halsey* who would have been adversely affected by the rezoning allowing multiple family housing near their homes, the League will be adversely affected by a decision allowing the auto salvage yard. The salvage yard is incompatible with the residential purpose for which the League was working to use the eighteen-block area. Not only will the salvage yard itself be detrimental, but a decision in Swift's favor will open the way for other commercial development in the eighteen-block area.
   The *Halsey* case also helps the League on the other two elements because it provides analogous facts. Concerning adequacy of representation, *Halsey* is similar in that the village did not purport to represent the interests of the property owners in the zoning matter, just as here the city has indicated that it may no longer represent the League's interest in developing the area for low income housing. Concerning timeliness, *Halsey* is similar because the property owners in that case filed suit only three weeks after suit was brought, while the League would intervene only a week or two after the city attorney's statement that the city might be wrong.

4.   The city will argue that the language of the statute supports its position:

   ►   The League's application is not "timely." Swift filed suit six months ago, immediately following the denial of its rezoning request. Six months is too long to wait.

   ►   The League has not established that its interest is or may be inadequately represented. First, the city has the responsibility to represent the interests of its people, including the members of the League. The city has not indicated that it has abandoned the plan advocated by the League; rather it has indicated that it will represent the people, not narrow special interest groups.

▶ The League would not be "bound" by an adverse judgment in this action because the court is not being asked to adjudicate the League's rights or responsibilities.

Further, the city will argue that *Halsey* supports its position:

▶ Timeliness. The intervenors in *Halsey* filed their application within three weeks after the suit was filed, leading the court to conclude that their application was timely. Here, the League has waited six months to file its application. The requirement that an application be timely has not been met.

▶ Adequacy of representation. In *Halsey*, the court noted that the village did not purport to represent the interests of the landowners. Thus, the landowners had to intervene to ensure that their interests would be represented. Here, the city has stated that it represents everyone, including the League and its members. In addition, the city has not indicated that it is taking a position adverse to that of the League, only that it is carefully considering its position.

▶ "Bound by a judgment." In *Halsey* the intervention application was filed by nearby property owners whose quality of life and property values would be adversely affected by the proposed rezoning. The League neither owns nor occupies the property involved. As a result, its interest would not be substantially affected.

5. The policy behind the statute is to ensure that all parties with an interest in the outcome of an action are given a chance to be heard before they are bound by the outcome. This policy is evidenced both by the committee's comment and the court's liberal construction of the statute in favor of the property owners in *Halsey*. This right is so important that courts are given no discretion; if the requirements of the statute are met, the applicant must be allowed to intervene. Here, this policy can best be served by ensuring that all parties with an interest in the zoning of this eighteen-block parcel be heard before an irrevocable decision is made. The League has invested a significant amount of planning and negotiation in this project on behalf of its members, all of which will be nullified by a decision in Swift's favor.

6. The requirements of the statute and the committee's comment support its position. The comment indicates that the statute is intended to include "persons having interests so vital that they ought to have been made parties in the first place." Here, the League is neither a property owner nor a resident in the affected area. Its advocacy interest is not sufficient to support the application of the statute here.

7. Students may conclude either way, but they should be able to explain why they have decided that one side's argument is stronger than the other. It may be helpful to work through the Chapter 8 factors for at least one of these sub-issues.

Exercise 8-E

The factual and legal materials for this exercise are also used in Exercise 14-C(3).

1.   The relevant rule is in section 31, which prohibits:

  a.   anyone other than a campaign committee member
  b.   from contributing more than $1,000
  c.   to the campaign of the winner of a primary election for the office of governor
  d.   for any purpose
  e.   after the date of such primary election. Sec. 31 (a).

Members of the winner's "immediate family," which is defined as a "spouse, parent, brother, sister, son, or daughter," are exempt. Sec. 31 (b & c).

Alberts established that this provision prohibits contributions that retire the candidate's debt from the primary election, holding that the statute's language "for any purpose" must be read for its full meaning.

Questions 2 and 3 implicitly require students to screen "givens" from the problem. That direction might better be made explicit. It is given that:

  a.   Odegaard was not a member of his granddaughter's campaign committee.
  b.   He did contribute more than $1,000 to her campaign.
  c.   Francine Odegaard did win the primary election for governor.
  d.   The contribution was made after the primary election.

The issues are: (1) Whether Rolf Odegaard's $41,995 contribution violates Section 31(a) and (2) Whether Rolf Odegaard is a member of Francine Odegaard's "immediate family."

2.   Language of the Act supporting the committee:

  ►   Rolf Odegaard is a person other than a campaign committee member. His $41,995 contribution exceeds $1,000. He meets the statutory requirement that the contribution be "for any purpose" because he contributed the money to retire a campaign debt.

  ►   Rolf Odegaard is not a spouse, parent, brother, sister, son, or daughter. Because he is not a member of Francine Odegaard's immediate family, he is not exempt from the $1,000 limit under section 31(b).

Facts of the cases supporting the committee:

  ►   The court in *Alberts* indicated that the language "for any purpose" includes the purpose of retiring campaign debts. Just as the contribution in *Alberts* was intended to retire a campaign debt, Odegaard here obviously was attempting to retire his granddaughter's campaign debt.

➤ The *Toland* court said that the immediate family exemption would ordinarily apply to the candidate's son, one of the types of persons specifically identified in section 31(b). Because a grandfather is not a listed family member, Rolf Odegaard does not qualify for the exemption.

3. Language of the Act supporting Rolf Odegaard:

➤ Section 31(a) applies to the winner of a primary election, not to the winner of a general election. This type of argument suggests, as students will see from the difficulty they have with this part of the question, that it is hard to make an argument for Rolf Odegaard based on the statutory language.

➤ Although he never formally adopted Francine, he raised her from early childhood after her parents died. He is also her grandfather, not an unrelated adoptive parent. Rolf Odegaard is thus part of her "immediate family" under section 31(c).

Facts of the cases supporting Rolf Odegaard:

➤ Section 31 has never been applied to contributions made after a general election. Thus, this situation is distinguishable from that in *Alberts*. The reasoning in that case—that large contributions near the end of a campaign can gain an improper level of influence for the contributor—is not applicable when the election has already been won.

➤ *Toland* is not applicable here. In that case, the candidate's son contributed money he had received from others. The court held that the immediate family exemption did not apply when a family member was merely a "conduit" for other people's money. In this case, by contrast, Rolf Odegaard donated his own money.

4. Policies supporting the committee:

➤ Section 2 of the Act is intended to regulate campaign financing, and to do so without jeopardizing candidates' ability to run effective campaigns. The section 31 restrictions will not adversely affect Francine Odegaard's ability to run an effective campaign because she has already won.

The committee will find additional policy support from the cases. Although the policy of improving the integrity of the election process may not be at issue, the appearance of integrity of the election process noted in *Alberts* is applicable here, as it is with any large donation.

Students may identify other policies not specifically stated in the Act or cases. The Act purports to put all candidates on a level playing field, for example. Thus, any exceptions to its application should be narrowly construed.

5. Policies supporting Odegaard:

The policy of regulating political activity set out in section 2 is inapplicable here because Odegaard did not make this donation for any political favors. Because he is the candidate's grandfather, the policies articulated in *Alberts* regarding the integrity or appearance of integrity of the election process are also inapplicable. Further, the policies behind the immediate family exception recognized in *Toland* apply here because he stands in the place of the candidate's parents. It would not be fair to deprive Francine Odegaard of her grandfather's support and yet allow other candidates the benefit of the support of their parents.

6. Rolf Odegaard is highly unlikely to prevail on the issue concerning section 31(a) spending limits. Students may decide the "immediate family" issue either way. This second issue comes down to the "letter of the law" versus the underlying policy. However they resolve these issues, they should be able to explain their position clearly.

9
Reaching a Conclusion

Changes From the Second Edition

There are no significant changes from the second edition.

Teaching Notes

In our experience, students find it easier to compare and contrast than to draw conclusions. This chapter is intended to help solve that problem. We have tried to provide guidance without being mechanical.

Some teachers find it useful to teach this chapter in conjunction with Chapters 7 (Common Law Analysis) and 8 (Statutory Analysis). The fifth step in each of those chapters requires students to draw a conclusion and defend it, and specifically urges students to refer to Chapter 9. One approach to classroom teaching is to work through each factor in this Chapter with the textual problems in Chapters 7 and 8.

Suggested Approach to Exercises

Most of the exercises in the book can be used to teach this chapter. We also use closed memorandum assignments that the students are working on or have just completed.

Exercise 9-A

The factual and legal materials for this exercise are also used in Exercises 11-A and 12-A.

What follows are suggested answers. There may be more here than you can use or want to use. We include it to provide a reasonably complete analysis of the problem.

First principle: A position is stronger to the extent that it involves little or no extension of existing law.

Issue 1: Was there a valid offer?

McKay: No. I didn't intend to make an offer. I was only joking and any reasonable person would have known it was a joke to offer a $100,000 yacht for $10,000. Green admitted as much when he said, "You can't be serious." This case is analogous to the offer in *Derek*, which the court found invalid because the offeree knew or should have known the offer was a practical joke.

Green: Yes. I had no reason to know that McKay was joking. I expressed surprise when I said "You can't be serious" but not disbelief that the offer was genuine, because immediately after that I asked for time to consider the offer and raise the money. This case is different from *Derek* because in that case the offeree knew the offeror's reputation as a practical joker. I did not know McKay had such a reputation.

Resolution of this issue depends on a straightforward application of the rule in *Derek*. Did Green know or should he have known that the offer was not serious? The facts can be read to favor either side. *Derek* is distinguishable, however, because the offeree in that case knew the reputation of the offeror. For this reason, the first factor tips slightly in Green's favor. A decision for McKay would call for a slight extension of existing law.

Issue 2: Was there a valid acceptance?

McKay: No. Green accepted the alleged offer on the condition that I include my golf clubs, a condition that was not part of the original offer. Because the acceptance did not mirror the offer in every respect, it is invalid. In this respect, this case is similar to *Anselm*, where the court held that a buyer's reply to a seller's offer agreeing to the seller's terms but changing the delivery dates was a counteroffer, not an acceptance.

Even if the acceptance was valid in form, it was not sufficiently communicated. When Green made his oral acceptance over the telephone, I did not hear it because I was unconscious. This case differs from *Anselm* in that regard. In *Anselm* the court considered delivery of a written acceptance sufficient even though the offeror had not read it. The offeree had done all that was required of him by delivering the written acceptance to the offeror's secretary. Green did not do all that was required of him. He should have realized when I did not respond that I had not heard his part of the conversation.

Green: Yes. I called McKay and said the words "I accept" right after he answered the phone. That was my acceptance. After that, I asked him to throw in his golf clubs, just to see how far he would go. Unlike the offeree in *Anselm*, I did not make the golf clubs a condition to accepting the yacht contract. It was just a suggestion.

Also, under the Uniform Commercial Code, which most states have adopted, there is no mirror-image rule. My suggestion about the golf clubs would be a proposal for an addition to the contract, not a counteroffer or rejection.

My acceptance was also sufficiently communicated. In *Anselm*, the court said that placement of written acceptance on the offeror's cluttered desk was sufficient. The offeree need not ensure that the offeror read it. Similarly, I gave my acceptance plainly over the telephone. I had no duty to ensure that McKay heard it.

McKay must argue that Green's golf club "suggestion" is really a condition, and it is phrased as such because it includes the conjunction "but." Neither McKay's argument that the golf club reference is a condition, and thus a counteroffer, nor Green's argument that it is a mere suggestion requires an extension of existing law. Both interpretations are possible according to the rules in *Anselm*, but the interpretation offered by McKay is more plausible. Green's argument for adoption of the UCC rule would be a change in the law and weakens his position. As to this sub-issue, McKay's position is stronger.

Green's argument that his communication was sufficient according to *Anselm* requires some extension of the law. A court might be reluctant to equate a telephone conversation with a drunken acquaintance to a properly delivered written communication to a business associate, despite some similarities. (In each case, the offeree delivered the message, but the message was not received.) McKay has a slight advantage here because Green's argument requires the court to stretch the *Anselm* case to cover quite different facts.

Issue 3: Was there sufficient consideration?

> McKay: No. The court in *Derek* stated the rule that the consideration must not be "so grossly disproportionate that it would shock the conscience of the court to enforce the contract." A payment of ten percent of the value of a $100,000 yacht would shock the conscience of the court.

> Green: Yes. The accepted rule is that any consideration, no matter how small, will support a contract.

The initial problem here is not whether one side requires an extension of existing law, but what the law is. McKay relies on dicta in the *Derek* majority opinion. Green relies on a statement in the dissenting opinion in *Derek* in which the judge cites a treatise on contract law. Assuming the majority stated the existing rule, McKay's argument fits squarely within it and his position would be quite strong.

Second principle: A position is stronger to the extent that it furthers the policies or purposes of the law.

The policy arguments made here could apply to any of the issues or sub-issues in this exercise.

> McKay: The purpose of contract law is to enforce serious agreements freely entered into by the parties, not to turn a joke between friends into an enforceable contract. I didn't freely enter into this contract because I made the offer in jest.

> Green: The purpose of contract law is to give effect to the reasonable expectations of the parties. My expectations were reasonable under the circumstances.

Although both parties have stated valid purposes for judicial enforcement of a contract, McKay's position is weak because the test in this jurisdiction is one of reasonableness. Therefore, his subjective intent is irrelevant. Furthermore, we know from the *Derek* case that the court will enforce an agreement that is also a practical joke if the requirements for a valid contract are met.

Third principle: When the law does not require a particular result, a position is stronger to the extent that it involves a fair or just outcome for the parties.

The fairness arguments made here could apply to any of the issues or sub-issues in this exercise.

> McKay: Enforcement of this alleged contract would be unfair because I would be losing $90,000 and Green would gain an unfair and undeserved benefit—a yacht for one-tenth of what it is worth.

Green: Enforcement of this contract is fair because McKay initiated the negotiations for sale by calling me and offering to sell his yacht. He can't complain now about unfairness because he led me to believe he was serious.

One view of justice is that McKay carried the joke too far, raised Green's expectations unnecessarily, and should now follow through with his part of the bargain. Another view is that Green would be getting a windfall if McKay is forced to sell Green his yacht for a fraction of its value. Both views are defensible, but McKay's position is probably stronger because Green has not suffered any monetary detriment.

According to this summary, McKay's position is stronger than Green's. Green has a less than even chance of proving all three elements of a contract, and neither the purposes of the law nor the considerations of fairness and justice clearly favor either side.

Exercise 9-B

The factual and legal materials for this exercise are also used in Exercises 11-B and 12-B.
Some arguments that students may raise under each guideline follow, but these are not meant to be exhaustive. Many of the arguments are described in this manual for Exercise 6-B. You may find it helpful to appoint half the class to represent one side and half to represent the other and then discuss how each of the factors would apply. When students are given a "client" they sometimes find it easier to see the arguments involved.

Issue 1. Does the exemption set out in section 5(a) apply to the police department records regarding the CLO?

First principle: A position is stronger to the extent that it involves little or no extension of existing law.

Banner-Patriot: These records do not deal with the "detection and investigation of crime." Even if they are maintained for the Police Department's internal use "in matters relating to law enforcement," they are analogous to the reports the court found not to be privileged in *Wheeler*. In *Wheeler*, the court held that a police department could not withhold reports concerning the offense committed, surrounding circumstances, witnesses, and investigating officers. The CLO records contain similar kinds of basic information.

Police Department: The exemption set out in 5(a) applies to the CLO files. The information in the CLO files is analogous to the Supplementary Offense Reports in *Wheeler*. To disclose this information would jeopardize the ongoing effort to investigate criminal activities as well as potentially revealing the names of informants. The paper is not seeking information about specific crimes, as was contained in the Offense Reports in *Wheeler*, but rather is seeking general information about an organization that may or may not be involved in criminal activity.

This factor probably favors the Police Department because these records are "internal records and notations" of the Department's internal use "related to law enforcement." In addition, the records are more analogous to the records that the *Wheeler* court said could be withheld.

Second principle: A position is stronger to the extent that it furthers the policies and purposes of the law.

Banner-Patriot: The policy behind the Freedom of Information Act is to ensure that the press and the public can know what activities their governing bodies are engaged in. We do not live in a society where the government is allowed to conduct its business in secret. This information was gathered by public servants and belongs to the public. The CLO is potentially a very destructive force in the community, and it derives some of its power from its secrecy. The community needs to be informed of its activities and the individuals involved.

Police Department: The public's access to information must be balanced with the Department's need to keep certain information confidential. The Freedom of Information Act was not intended to hamper law enforcement efforts or jeopardize the safety of police informants. That is why the exception in 5(a) was included in the statute.

The Police Department's argument that disclosure would interfere with an ongoing investigation is likely to outweigh the newspaper's public information argument.

Third principle: When the law does not require a particular result, a position is stronger to the extent that it involves a fair or just outcome for the parties.

Banner-Patriot: The press has a responsibility to keep its readers informed about important matters in their community. The CLO may be a threat to individuals or the community as a whole, but a story about the CLO is difficult to write because of the secrecy with which the organization conducts its affairs. The police files might contain information that the paper will not be able to obtain any other way and which is crucial to any story it may write.

Police Department: The Department has invested two years in investigating the CLO, an investigation that is not concluded as yet. To disclose the information sought would place all of the effort expended to this point in jeopardy. If and when arrests are made, the paper will receive the pertinent information.

The fairness argument comes down a question of timing. So long as the investigation is continuing, and there is a reasonable suspicion of illegal activity (as there is here), withholding the information is probably the fairest result at present.

As a result, we think the Police Department could justify refusing to disclose the records under section 5(a). We recognize that students might draw a contrary conclusion, reasoning, for example, that the Police Department "investigation" is really just an ongoing monitoring activity of a suspicious organization. Those students should be asked to explain, however, why such an investigation doesn't increase the likelihood of detecting criminal activity that the organization directly or indirectly encourages.

Issue 2. Does the exemption set out in section 5(d) apply to the police department records regarding the CLO?

First principle (existing law):

This factor probably tips in favor of the Police Department because of the sweeping nature of the newspaper's request and because the investigation is not yet completed. Investigations like this usually involve people who are likely to be guilty of wrongdoing as well as people who are suspected but are ultimately innocent. If it received the Department's files, the newspaper would have information about people who have not committed any crime and who do not intend to do so; using such information might constitute an invasion of their privacy. In addition, the police have obtained information about membership of the CLO. Mere membership in an organization does not ordinarily make that person a criminal, but disclosure of that information is likely to be embarrassing, although probably not a "clearly unwarranted invasion of privacy."

Second principle (policies and purposes):

The purpose of the section 5(d) exemption is evident from its adoption only two years after the *Holcombe* case. The newspaper will argue that those who voluntarily join a paramilitary organization with racist views are in a radically different position from that of a rape victim. On the other hand, without knowing who has been investigated (other than the mayor's wife), and what information is in the files, it is impossible to say that only bad or guilty people will turn up in the police records. For that reason, this factor also favors the Department.

Third principle (fair or just outcome):

Not disclosing the information is fair to the innocent people who are being, or who have been, investigated. This result gives the Police Department an opportunity to finish a proper investigation. Presumably, the people who have committed crimes will be charged, so the fact that their names and activities are not now disclosed is unimportant.

Thus, the section 5(d) exemption applies. This may be surprising to students, and there may be some discussion about whether the files could somehow be divided. Some students may see this as one of those problems where you reduce the scope of a sweeping request to get at least some of what you want. A teacher could generate an interesting discussion by asking how that could be done effectively.

Part C
Basic Concepts of Legal Writing

10
Organization

Changes From the Second Edition

We added a new rule on overall organization: When there is more than one issue, discuss them in a logical order. We also changed the example illustrating rule 4.

Teaching Notes

The chapters in Part C build in a logical order to Chapters 14 (Drafting the Discussion) and 15 (Revising and Editing). Some teachers may find it helpful to teach these chapters in sequence, and some may find it helpful to skip some of these chapters and then return to them. We have, for example, taught Chapters 10, 14, and 15 early in the year, and then returned to Chapters 11, 12, and 13 later. Some of the chapters in this section can also be taught together in a longer class. Chapters 10 (Organization) and 14 (Drafting the Discussion) work well together. Chapters 13 (Signposting) and 15 (Revising and Editing) can be used together very effectively during a class where students edit a piece of work. Students can work on a sample that you provide, or you may ask them to perform a peer- or a self-edit related to the writing project they are working on. You can then return to these same chapters when students are working on other projects later in the year.

We wrote this chapter in response to recurring problems in student papers. This chapter is the first in Part C because it provides a structure within which the lessons in the other chapters fit. Because good organization is fundamental, many teachers find this chapter and its exercises worth emphasizing.

Suggested Approach to Exercises

Exercise 10-A

The factual and legal materials for this exercise are also used in Exercise 17-A.

Students find this problem interesting because it offers a choice of rules. The will could be invalid under the *Steffans* test, the *Kendall* test, or both. It is also a good problem for getting students to identify facts relevant to the elements in each test and to make arguments based on these facts.

1.   Students should have no difficulty identifying the two rules and their elements from the cases. Because both rules involve undue influence, the best descriptive labels for the rules may be based on the case names (*e.g.*, *Kendall* rule).

If you use this exercise for an in-class discussion, this would be a good place to use an elements chart. Here is one approach:

Steffans Rule ELEMENTS CHART		
Element	**Facts of our case**	**Elements met**
Susceptibility to undue influence	Colonel was vice-president of company. Before he wrote his second will, company financed foreign trips for him, allegedly to learn foreign land development strategies.	Maybe
Opportunity to influence	Colonel went on frequent fishing trips with company's general counsel. General counsel drafted the second will.	Yes
Disposition to influence	General counsel worked for the company.	Maybe
Coveted result	Second will gave Colonel's entire estate to the company, but general counsel may have wanted to benefit personally.	Maybe

You may want to add a fourth column to this chart showing the relevant facts for each element in the *Steffans* case. You might point out that although the court is far from explicit in its holding on each element, you can infer the holding on specific elements from the facts. The pertinent facts are identified in the outline under question 5.

The other elements chart might look like this:

Element	Facts of our case	Element met?
Kendall Rule ELEMENTS CHART		
Element	**Facts of our case**	**Element met?**
Confidential relationship between testator and one alleged to have exercised under influence (that is, whether the confidant controlled or influenced drafting of the will)	Person who wrote second will was Colonel's personal attorney, and was general counsel for the company where Colonel was vice-president.	Maybe
Suspicious circumstances surrounding making of will	In second will, Colonel gave his entire estate to the company. General counsel went on frequent fishing trips with Colonel. Not clear how or whether general counsel benefited personally.	Yes

Again, you might want to add a fourth column showing the relevant facts from the *Kendall* case. The pertinent facts are identified in the outline under question 5.

2.   Using this analysis, the issues and sub-issues break out like this:

(1)   Whether the general counsel exercised undue influence (under the *Steffans* test).
   a.   Whether the Colonel was susceptible to undue influence.
   b.   Whether the general counsel had a disposition to influence.
   c.   Whether the general counsel obtained the coveted result.
(2)   Whether there were a confidential relationship between the general counsel and the Colonel (under the *Kendall* test) (that is, whether the general counsel controlled or influenced drafting of the will).

3.   The plausible arguments for and against your client's position on each issue and sub-issue are indicated by the facts stated in the charts.

4.   Drawing a conclusion, again, is harder for students than making arguments for either side. This is a good place to reinforce the three factors from Chapter 8 (Reaching a Conclusion). You might take one or more issues or sub-issues and work through the factors one at a time.

5.   Here is one approach to outlining the analysis:

(1)   Court would probably not hold the second will invalid under the *Steffans* test.
   a.   Opportunity to influence. Attorney and Colonel had much contact. *Steffans* distinguishable because there was no contact.
   b.   Disposition to influence. General counsel knew company would benefit. *Steffans* distinguishable because paperboy had no idea he would benefit.
   c.   General counsel probably received coveted result. Company benefited, and that would help him. *Steffans* is analogous, even though benefit is not as direct.
   d.   Colonel probably not susceptible to undue influence. Like the woman's will in *Steffans*, his will is unusual. But he was not senile, he was estranged from the son who would have benefited from the first will, and he appears to have been devoted to the company.

(2)   Court would probably not hold the will invalid under the *Kendall* test.
   a.   General counsel probably did not control or influence drafting of the will. Drafter of second will was Colonel's personal attorney as well as general counsel for company. Unlike *Kendall*, Colonel was active, not senile. Fact that general counsel drafted will that benefited his company does not mean that the Colonel didn't make this decision.
   b.   Suspicious circumstances surrounding making of the will. Analogy to *Kendall*, because attorney there was personal attorney for beneficiary's mother. Company received entire estate based on will drafted by general counsel.

Exercise 10-B

The factual and legal materials for this problem are also used in Exercises 17-A, 18-B, and 19-B.

1.   There are three relevant rules: the regulation, nuisance, and trespass. Some students want to argue that the farmers should sue the Department of the Environment under section 11 for not promulgating a more protective regulation, especially when they find that the regulation does not apply. But the problem focuses on possible causes of action against the company, not against the agency.

As in the previous exercise, elements charts help clarify the analysis. Section 14 allows any person to bring an action in the appropriate trial court to enforce the regulations.

An elements chart for the regulation might look like this:

Regulation ELEMENTS CHART		
Element	**Facts of our case**	**Element met?**
Powerhouse with capacity of more than 500,000 pounds of steam per hour.	Powerhouse has capacity of 500,000 pounds of steam per hour.	No, although students will want to say "maybe."
Burns fuel that exceeds 1.0% sulfur content by weight.	Burns coal containing 0.9% to 1.2% by weight.	Yes, at least some of the time.

Students find the first element challenging, and many will look for reasons it should apply. Some may argue, for example, that the powerhouse could not possibly have a capacity of exactly 500,000 pounds per hour, using technical reasons. Based on the facts in the problem, however, the regulation is not applicable.

An elements chart for nuisance based on the Hancock case might look like this:

Nuisance ELEMENTS CHART		
Element	**Facts of our case**	**Element met?**
Defendant landowner	All-Rite owns land on which factory is located or a lease-hold estate in the land. Factory emits sulfur dioxide.	Yes
Unreasonably	Although there is interference, All-Rite employs 490 people and provides much income for community. Coal has lower sulfur content than coal burned in other states.	Maybe
Interferes with use and enjoyment	Sulfur dioxide reduces value of farmer's crops by 5%, reduces value of their property by $5,000 to $10,000, and probably increases their respiratory ailments.	Yes
Of the plaintiff's land	Farmers' land is affected.	Yes

Notice that the facts under the first element are inferred from the problem. This might be a useful place to talk about when it is permissible to draw inferences from the factual situation. In this case, is any other inference possible? We think not.

As in Exercise 10-A, you might want to develop a fourth column for the facts of the *Peters* case. The pertinent facts are identified in the outline under Question 5 of this exercise.

An elements chart for trespass based on the *Neely* and *Jacobs* cases might look like this:

Trespass ELEMENTS CHART		
Element	**Facts of our case**	**Element met?**
Physical invasion - some tangible object	Sulfur dioxide settles on fields. It is emitted into the air.	Maybe
by the defendant	All-Rite emits sulfur dioxide.	Yes
on the plaintiff's land	Sulfur dioxide settles on farmers' land.	Yes
Unless privileged by necessity	There are no facts to show that it is economically unfeasible for All-Rite to further reduce emissions.	Maybe

Because there are two relevant cases, it may be worthwhile to prepare case briefing charts for the two sub-issues in this problem.

2.   The problem thus suggests the following issues and sub-issues:
    (1)   Whether All-Rite's interference with the use and enjoyment of the farmers' property is unreasonable and therefore a nuisance.
    (2)   Whether All-Rite's sulfur dioxide emissions trespass on the farmers' land.
        a.   Whether the sulfur dioxide emissions are tangible and therefore physically invade the farmers' land.
        b.   Whether All-Rite's emissions are privileged by necessity.

3.   The plausible arguments for and against your client's position on each issue and sub-issue are indicated by the facts stated in the charts.

4.   As stated earlier, it is harder for students to draw conclusions than to make arguments for either side. This is a good place to reinforce the three factors from Chapter 8 (Reaching a Conclusion). You might take one or more issues or sub-issues and work through the factors one at a time.

5.   Here is one approach to outlining the analysis (with the elements rearranged in some cases to make the analysis more understandable):
    (1)   The regulation does not apply. Even though powerhouse burns coal containing more than 1.0% sulfur content by weight at least part of the time, the powerhouse does not have a capacity of more than 500,000 pounds of steam per hour.
    (2)   All-Rite is causing a nuisance.
        a.   All-Rite, the would-be defendant, is a landowner; it either owns the property in fee simple or it owns a leasehold estate in the property. All-Rite is like the saloon owner in *Peters*.

b.   The farmers who would be the plaintiffs are also landowners. They are like the homeowner in *Peters*.

c.   All-Rite has interfered with the use and enjoyment of their land because the powerhouse's emissions have reduced the value of the farmer's crops by 5%, reduced the value of their property by $5,000 to $10,000, and probably increased their respiratory ailments. This interference is analogous to, but more serious than, the disturbances caused by the saloon's patrons in *Peters*.

d.   All-Rite's interference is unreasonable. *Peters* is distinguishable because it involved only occasional loudness or rudeness by the saloon's patrons. All-Rite's interference involves reduced crop and property values as well as the likelihood of respiratory ailments. In *Peters*, the court said the defendant should do what she could, but suggested that her patrons were not under her control. In this case, by contrast, All-Rite's emissions are entirely under its control. The facts in this problem do not suggest that All-Rite is doing everything it could; it might, for example, increase the height of its stack or use lower sulfur coal. All-Rite's apparent compliance with the regulation and the jobs and money it contributes to the local economy do not mean it is doing everything it can.

(3)   All-Rite's emissions are trespassing on the farmers' land.

a.   The sulfur dioxide emissions constitute a physical invasion of the farmer's land because they settle on their alfalfa fields. *Neely* is distinguishable because it involves light, not a chemical compound (albeit a gaseous one) that can settle on leaves.

        [Students will argue this sub-issue both ways, and will characterize sulfur dioxide in different ways in so doing. The problem does not state whether sulfur dioxide is a gas or a particle. Some students, of course, will provide answers based on their knowledge of chemistry or environmental pollution. You might use that to explain the importance of further factual research in real-world legal situations.]

b.   The invasion is by All-Rite, the would-be defendant. In that respect, this case is analogous to *Neely*.

c.   The emissions invade the farmers' land. The farmers are like the homeowner in *Neely*.

d.   The invasion is probably not privileged by necessity. The car driver in *Jacobs* was trying to save his own life. In this case, there is no claim that All-Rite's emissions are driven by economic necessity, much less the necessity of saving lives.

11
Describing the Law

Changes From the Second Edition

We changed the example under rule 4 due to changes in the law. Exercise 11-C is new.

Teaching Notes

Deciding how much information to include about a case or statute and whether to quote or paraphrase are often difficult decisions for beginning law students. Some of us hand out an outline, similar to the one below, that summarizes these and other topics discussed in this chapter and offers additional examples drawn from the examples and exercises in the text or from a recent assignment.

1. Be accurate.

    Accuracy is essential in legal writing because without it you have no credibility. There are four kinds of inaccuracy:
    (a) *Misstating the law or the facts.* An obvious error is representing as the holding of the court a statement that is dicta, Another is representing as the rule in the case a rule that the court rejected. Careful reading of the cases and checking your case briefs for congruency (chapter 3) will eliminate these kinds of errors.
    (b) *Giving an incomplete rule of law,* as illustrated by Answer A in the first example in Part 1 and Answer C in the second example. In Answer A, the writer left out at least one requirement of the remedy of specific performance. In Answer C, the writer omitted important information regarding the notice requirement. It is always better to quote rather than paraphrase the relevant portions of a rule.
    (c) *Lack of precision in stating the law,* as illustrated by Answer A also. The writer said "fair" consideration but the rule laid down by the court said "adequate." These two terms may not have the same meaning or legal significance. Avoid elegant variation in legal writing.
    (d) *Failing to show how various elements relate to each other,* also illustrated by Answer A. The element of inadequate remedy at law includes unascertainable damages and unique items. They are not three separate elements.

    Example: Assume that in your state, burglary is defined as "breaking and entering the dwelling of another with the intent to commit a felony therein." Consider this description of the law:

    > One who breaks into the dwelling of another and has the intent to commit a felony has committed burglary.

    This description demonstrates three of the four kinds of inaccuracy.

- ▶ It is incomplete. Two elements, "entering" and "therein," are missing.

- ▶ It is imprecise. The writer might have intended the term "breaks into" to include both breaking and entering, but we cannot know for sure. This is an example of altering the language of a rule unnecessarily.

- ▶ It does not show how the elements relate to each other. Two relationships are not included: (1) One must have, <u>at the time of the breaking and entering</u>, an intent to commit a felony. The intent element is not met if the actor forms the intent after breaking and entering. (2) There must be an intent to commit a felony inside the dwelling, not somewhere else.

2.   <u>Describe only the relevant law.</u>

Whether you are using a statute or common law, include only the parts directly relevant to the issue under discussion. For example, if the *Lopez* case on page 134 addressed all of the requirements for specific performance, and you were discussing only the element of inadequacy of a remedy at law, you would describe only the facts, holding, and reasoning related to the inadequacy issue. Similarly, if you were analyzing the offer issue in Exercise 6-A and describing *Derek v. Beir*, you would not include the statements in the majority and dissenting opinions regarding consideration in that section of your paper.

3.   <u>Describe the law in enough detail.</u>

There is no set rule regarding how much detail to include. A good rule of thumb is this: The reader should not have to read the law (the case or statute) to follow your discussion and understand your logic. To put it another way, your paper should be self-contained. [Beginning legal writing students sometimes overlook this rule because the professor gives them the law they are to use, so they assume the reader (the professor) is familiar with it; therefore, they can just refer to it. Remind them that in real life, the reader may not have read the cases or statutes and should be able to rely on the writer's description.]

As the example in Part 3 illustrates, including the reasoning of a court is often necessary for a clear understanding of the issue and holding. Facts are also necessary in some instances to put a rule or holding in context. In Exercise 7-C, for example, it is important to explain that the court's ruling in *Shover v. Scott* concerned the right to lateral support, a legal right quite different from the right at issue in Greenleaf's case.

4.   <u>Summarize the law whenever appropriate.</u>

How much information—when you must include the facts, holding, reasoning of a case—depends on what you are using the case for.

(a)   A bare citation with no facts, holding, etc. is appropriate if you are citing the case for an undisputed legal principle.

Example: The list of required elements for specific performance given in _Lopez_ on page 134. is sufficient if the definition of specific performance is not in controversy.

(b)   A full description of key facts, holding, and reasoning is necessary if the case is central to your analysis. Suppose you are analyzing the acceptance issue in Exercise 6-A. Since you will use the _Anselm_ facts, holding, and reasoning in your analysis, you would include them in your description of the law.

(c)   One sentence or a parenthetical is sufficient If you are using a case for a settled or collateral point.

Example: An item is unique if it cannot be duplicated or replaced. _Lopez_ (Picasso sketch unique because irreplaceable).

5.   <u>Synthesize the law whenever necessary</u>.

If several cases support a particular point, case synthesis results in a more coherent and cohesive picture of the law than a series of case summaries. By showing what the cases have in common, you can more easily compare them to or distinguish them from the facts of your case. Your synthesis should begin with a thesis statement. In the example below, assume that you are analyzing the falsity element of the libel issue in Chapter 7:

Minor or technical errors in a published statement are not enough to render the statement false. According to the court in _White v. Ball_, the test is whether "the gist, the sting, of the matter is false." In _White,_ the court held that a customer's statement accusing employees of stealing his watch was "substantially accurate" even though the watch had been stolen by an employee's friend, who had been present at the work site. Similarly, in _Willow v. Orr_, a statement by a woman that her husband had kidnapped their four-year-old son, while technically inaccurate, was "true in substance." The husband's act of taking the child without the wife's consent and traveling with him to another state was not kidnapping in the legal sense because the husband had not violated any custody orders, but the essence of the charge was true. [Following would be a discussion comparing these cases to Dooley's case.]

When the facts of the cases do not require much explanation, you may use a simplified synthesis consisting of a series of case citations with explanatory parentheticals.[8]

Example: [Preceding is a discussion of _Avery v._ Goth, (1985), in which the court rejected the common law rule that a landowner has no duty to prevent natural vegetation on his property from obscuring the view of motorists on an adjoining street or highway.] Several courts have adopted the _Avery_ rule. _See Costa v. Lockhart_ (2002) (foliage blocking view of street); _Daily v. Compton_ (1995) (tree near shopping mall exit); _Graves v. Hoffman_ (1987) (weeds on shoulder of road).

---

[8] The cases in this example were suggested by _Sprecher v. Adamson_, 636 P.2d 1121 (Cal. 1981); _Whitt v. Silverman_, 788 So. 2d 210 (Fla. 2001); and _Langden v. Rushton_, 360 N.W.2d 270 (Mich. Ct. App. 1984).

Suggested Approach to Exercises

Exercise 11-A

We include thesis sentences here to provide a structure for the description of the law. You may want your students to do the same.

After a thesis sentence or two stating that the contract is or is not enforceable, the discussion and the description of the law would progress from issue to issue. This is a typical thesis statement:

> The contract between McKay and Green is unenforceable. Although there was an effective offer, there was no valid acceptance, and the consideration is probably insufficient to support a contract.

Thereafter, the description of the law would be organized as follows: effective offer (law from *Derek*); valid acceptance (law from *Anselm*); adequate consideration (law from *Derek*).

Following are two examples of how to describe the law relevant to the offer issue based on different conclusions. In the first, the conclusion is that the offer was effective. In the second, the conclusion is that it was not. Notice that the only difference between the two suggested answers is the way the writer introduces the law. The lesson for students is that regardless of the conclusion, the writer must describe the law fairly and objectively. The support for the conclusion will come when the writer applies the law to the facts of the case.

Example 1

McKay made an effective offer to sell his yacht to Green because Green reasonably believed McKay intended to make a binding offer, even though McKay may not have actually had that intent. An offer is effective in this state if the offeror intended to make a binding offer, but intent is defined not by what the offeror actually intended but by an objective standard: "[W]hether a reasonable person in the offeree's shoes would believe that the offeror intended to make a binding contract." *Derek.* In *Derek*, the offeror told the offeree, his neighbor, that for five dollars he would build a wall between their lots so that he would never have to look at the offeree's "ridiculous" face again. The offeree agreed and paid him five dollars, but the offeror never built the fence. The offeree in that case knew about the offeror's reputation for playing practical jokes on his neighbors. Under those circumstances, the court held that there was no binding offer because the offeree either knew or should have known that the offeror was not serious.

[The next paragraph would distinguish *Derek* and show why Green's belief was reasonable.]

Example 2

McKay's offer to sell his yacht to Green is not enforceable because the offer was not effective. An effective offer is one in which the offeror intends to make a binding contract. *Derek.* Intent is defined not by what the offeror actually intended but by an objective standard: "[W]hether a reasonable person in the offeree's shoes would believe that the offeror intended to make a binding contract." *Derek*. In *Derek*, the offeror told the offeree, his neighbor, that for five dollars he would build a wall between their lots so that he would never have to look at the offeree's "ridiculous" face again. The offeree agreed and paid him five dollars, but the offeror never built the fence. The offeree in that case knew about the offeror's reputation for playing practical jokes on his neighbors. Under those circumstances, the court held that there was no binding offer because the offeree either knew or should have known that the offeror was not serious.

[The next paragraph would analogize the McKay case to *Derek* and show why Green should have known the offer was not serious even though he did not know of McKay's reputation as a practical joker.]

Exercise 11-B

The law in Exercise 6-B was based on the Freedom of Information Act and the *Wheeler Publishing* case. Much of the legal description for this exercise is based on the answers to Exercise 6-B. As in Exercise 11-A, you may want students to include thesis sentences to provide a structure for the discussion. The statute (especially sections 3 and 4 as well as the definitions) needs to be summarized in order to create a context for the exceptions. Section 5(a) should be quoted and the case explained. Then section 5(d) should be quoted.

Exercise 11-C

Students should first give the common law rule and then explain the exceptions in the context of the case law. Example:

Philip and Julia Langford have no property interest in the dogwood trees they planted in their backyard because the trees were part of the real estate they sold to Wilbur and Marcie Cliff. The common law rule is that trees growing in the soil are part of the land. *Dinesen v. Stafford Nat'l Bank*. There are two exceptions to this rule. The first exception is that crops are considered personal property if the owner so intended. *Id.* In *Dinesen*, the court held that cranberry bushes were not crops because the owner intended to harvest only the berries, not the bushes themselves. Therefore, the bushes were part of the realty.

[The next paragraph would analogize *Dinesen* and explain why the trees would probably not be considered crops.]

The second exception is that trees or plants that are stock in trade are the merchant's personal property. *Updike v. Teague*. Stock in trade is defined as "goods or chattel that a merchant obtains for the purpose of resale." *Id.* In *Updike*, the court held that young trees in a nursery were personal property, characterizing them as goods offered for sale that a merchant must temporarily store in the ground in order to keep them alive.

[The next paragraph would distinguish *Updike* on the basis that the trees were on private property and were not offered for sale at the time of the real estate transaction.]

12
Explaining the Analysis

Changes From the Second Edition

Exercise 12-C is new and gives students the opportunity to analyze an issue using two different theories, as illustrated in the example under Part 3.

Teaching Notes

Students often find it difficult to fully and completely explain how the relevant law applies to the specific facts of a new problem. It is not uncommon to see fairly good descriptions of the law followed by explanations that are brief, superficial, and conclusory. Some professors use non-legal examples to help their students learn how to draw specific analogies and distinctions. One professor always begins with the classic comparison between apples and oranges, setting two on the desk at the beginning of class. Students very quickly discover that apples and oranges have at least as many similarities as they have differences.

Encourage your students to compare and contrast all the relevant aspects of each case they read with the other cases and with the problem they are trying to resolve. You can create lists of similarities and differences on the board, or have students develop detailed case briefing charts and analysis charts, as shown in Chapters 7 (Common Law Analysis) and 8 (Statutory Analysis). Then, when students begin to explain their analysis of a legal question, they will have the specific information necessary to draw strong analogies and distinctions and explain the basis for their position on an issue.

Remind students that they must make the point of comparison explicit. The phrase "Like *Smith* . . ." is unclear because the writer has not identified the point of comparison between *Smith* and the present case. Statements such as "Like the defendant in *Smith* . . ." or "Like the search conducted in *Smith* . . ." identify the specific point of comparison and make the subsequent explanation of the writer's analysis easier to follow.

Suggested Approach to Exercises

Exercise 12-A

This exercise works best as a follow-up to Exercise 11-A. These answers continue the discussion begun in Exercise 11-A. The first answer concludes that there was an effective offer; the second concludes that there was not.

Example 1

McKay made an effective offer to sell his yacht to Green because Green reasonably believed McKay intended to make a binding offer, even though McKay may not have actually had that intent. [Here a description of the law in *Derek*.]

Unlike the offeree in *Derek*, Green did not know of McKay's reputation as a practical joker and so had no reason to doubt that the offer was genuine. His response at the end of the conversation that he needed time to think about the offer and raise the money shows that he took the offer seriously. This attitude was reasonable because McKay gave him no reason to doubt the sincerity of the offer. Green expressed incredulity at the beginning of the conversation when he said "You can't be serious" after McKay offered to sell his yacht at one-tenth of its value. But McKay continued the conversation after that and never intimated that the offer was a joke. Green's belief that McKay intended to make a binding offer was therefore reasonable under the circumstances.

Example 2

McKay's offer to sell his yacht to Green is not enforceable because the offer was not effective. [Here a description of the law in *Derek*.]

In *Derek*, the offeree sought to enforce a contract based on a practical joke. The court rejected that attempt, holding that the offeree knew or should have known that the offer was made in jest. This case is similar. As a joke, McKay offered to sell his $100,000 yacht to Green for $10,000. Even though Green did not know that McKay had a reputation as a practical joker, he should have known that the offer was a joke. He knew the true value of the boat and exclaimed "You can't be serious" when McKay made the offer. The court in *Derek* refused to enforce a contract when the offeror promised to build a wall between their adjoining lots for five dollars. In McKay's case, the difference in value between the subject of the offer and the price is also greatly disproportionate. Green may have actually believed that McKay intended to make a binding offer; he requested time to consider the offer and raise the money. If he had that belief, however, it was not reasonable under the circumstances.

Exercise 12-B

This exercise works best as a follow-up to Exercise 11-B.

Students should first explain all of the "givens," one by one. This explanation should show that the newspaper complied with section 3 and that an action to compel disclosure under section 4 is appropriate. Students should then explain why the text of section 5(a) does or does not apply to this case. This explanation needs to be accompanied by an explanation of how the *Wheeler Publishing* case is analogous to or different from the facts of this case. Finally, students need to explain why the text of section 5(d) does or does not apply to the *Banner-Patriot*'s case.

Exercise 12-C

This exercise works best as a follow-up to Exercise 11-C.

Students might reach different conclusions when they analyze the issue using both the crop theory and the stock-in-trade theory. They might decide, for example, that the trees are not crops but they are stock in trade. Even if they reach the conclusion that the trees are neither, and therefore no longer the property of the Langfords, it is important to explain the law and its application under both theories.

As to the first issue, whether the trees were crops, the likely conclusion is that they were not. The court in *Dinesen* pointed out that the cranberry bushes were not crops because only the berries, not the bushes, were harvested annually. Trees are also not harvested annually. Students might disagree about whether this issue a "given." Clearly, trees are not "crops" in the ordinary sense of the word. However, the trees in this case were intended to be harvested, in the sense that they were to be dug up and sold to customers. Students could therefore make a legitimate argument that *Dinesen* is distinguishable and the trees are similar to plants traditionally considered crops.

The second issue presents a closer question. The facts in this case are virtually identical to the facts in *Updike*—trees intended to be sold were temporarily stored by being planted in the ground. A reasonable conclusion is that, like the trees in *Updike*, they were stock in trade. The important difference is that the Langfords' trees were in the backyard of a private residence, not in a commercial nursery. Students should explain the relevance of this fact.

In analyzing both issues, students should recognize the importance that the courts placed on the owner's intent. The court In *Dinesen* stated that the owner must *intend* that plants growing in the soil are crops to be harvested. The court in *Updike* stated that stock in trade is property that the merchant obtains *for the purpose of* resale. If other considerations are evenly balanced, intent is often the deciding factor.

13
Signposting

Changes From the Second Edition

In Part 3, we clarified the difference between topic and thesis sentences.

Teaching Notes

The exercises in this chapter can be used for collaborative work in class as long as the groups remain quite small—perhaps two or three students. As mentioned at the beginning of Part C, this chapter also works well as a vehicle for a self-editing or peer-editing exercise, using the four principles set out in the chapter as a checklist.

Suggested Approach to Exercises

Exercise 13-A

This exercise works best if you tell students in advance what to look for. The discussion needs a thesis statement, topic sentences for the paragraphs, transitions between cases, and a transition between the cases and your client's facts. Some students will rewrite this exercise entirely unless you limit them to specific problems. You may want a total rewrite, but you should say so if you do not. To focus your students' attention, you can use the Teacher's Manual CD to create a handout of this exercise, inserting spaces or empty text boxes at the places in the discussion where signposts are needed.

This is an example of how we might correct the specific problems described above. Additions are in boldface.

> **Although McGraw used a cane that resembled a gun during the robbery, he did not use it in a manner likely to cause harm. He is therefore not likely to be convicted of armed robbery.** A person commits armed robbery when, with intent to commit theft, he takes the property of another by use of an "offensive weapon." State Code § 365(b). The courts have defined "offensive weapon" as including not only a weapon *per se* but also anything used in a manner likely to cause death or great bodily injury. *Fann v. State*; *Meminger v. State*.
>
> **McGraw's cane was not a weapon *per se*.** In both *Fann* and *Choate* the defendants used replicas of guns to commit robberies. The court held in both cases that the defendants could not be convicted of armed robbery because the legislature had specifically eliminated statutory language that would have brought replicas within the purview of the armed robbery statute. Like the defendants in *Fann* and *Choate*, McGraw cannot be convicted of armed robbery simply because he used something that looked like a gun.

In addition, McGraw's use of the cane was not likely to cause death or great bodily injury. For example, in *Fann* there was no evidence that the defendant tried to strike the victim; in *Choate* the defendant was unable to do so because the victim was seated in an enclosed booth. In both cases the court noted the lack of any evidence of an intent to harm the victim. Similarly, McGraw did not attempt to hit the owner, or show any intent to do so.

Although some facts indicate that McGraw may have intended to strike the coin shop owner, a court is unlikely to conclude that he had that intent. Unlike the defendant in *Fann*, who gave no indication of intent to strike the victim, McGraw did swing the weapon back and forth menacingly and did threaten to "hurt [the shop owner] bad" unless he cooperated. Also, the shop owner stated that he was fearful of being either shot or struck, indicating the weapon's movement implied this threat. However, the court in *Fann* did not infer an intention to harm without substantive indication of such intent. The court is unlikely to find swinging the cane back and forth sufficient to establish McGraw's intent to strike the shop owner when McGraw made no attempt to do so. Therefore, because McGraw did not use the cane in a manner indicating an intent to harm the shop owner, he is not likely to be convicted of armed robbery.

The *Meminger* case, in which the court found that the defendant showed an intent to cause harm, is distinguishable. In *Meminger*, the defendant was convicted of armed robbery when he hit the victim in the head with a liquor bottle. The court held that because the bottle was used in a manner likely to cause harm, it was an offensive weapon. McGraw, on the other hand, did not use the cane in a way indicating an intent to hit the shop owner; he only swung the cane back and forth and did not swing it at the owner. **Thus, because the cane is not likely to be considered an offensive weapon, McGraw did not commit armed robbery.**

Exercise 13-B

Try to direct your students to edit what is here and not to completely rewrite the analysis.

You might explain to your students that there are cases saying that there is no release from negligence unless the release specifically refers to negligence. Those cases are analyzed in the discussion of the counterargument, which is not included in this excerpt. That is why the text states that the issue is whether the word "negligence" must be specifically included in the release to bar an action for negligence.

This paragraph needs to be divided into several paragraphs. Additionally, it needs a thesis statement, topic sentences for the new paragraphs, and transitions between the cases and your facts. In the example below, additions are in boldface and deletions are in brackets.

The court will likely conclude that the release Spencer signed bars any action for negligence against the outfitter, even though it does not mention negligence. Although the courts of this state have not addressed this issue, they have held that releases must be interpreted to mean what they say. The court in *Conner*, **for example**, held that a release was invalid and did not bar a cause of action arising from a motorcycle accident at a racetrack. The release purported to absolve the defendant from liability, but it mentioned only "automobile racing" in a list of racing activities included. The court reasoned that motorcycle racing was not included under the commonly understood definition of automobile racing.

The court in *Anders* also indicated that a release must be read according to its plain language. [In *Anders*], the court granted summary judgment to the defendant after the plaintiff sued for damages arising from the defendant's negligence in drilling oil and gas wells. The contract between the parties specifically absolved the defendant from liability arising from its negligence. **However**, the court based its decision on the equal bargaining positions of the parties and the unequivocal language of the contract.

Although both cases interpret releases according to their plain words, neither *Conner* nor *Anders* [did not address] addressed the specific question presented here **because** the contract between Spencer and Rocky River Outfitters (RRO) [however] did not contain the word "negligence."

The courts in other states have applied the same plain-language principle as this state's courts, holding that broadly worded releases bar negligence actions even if they do not use that word. For example, the courts in *Sommers* and *Cabel* concluded that specific mention of the word "negligence" was not necessary if the intent of the parties was otherwise clearly expressed. The release in *Sommers* absolved a parachuting school from "any and all claims, demands, actions . . . whatsoever, in any way resulting from personal injuries . . . arising from . . . parachute jumping." **Similarly,** in *Cabel* the release covered "any and all losses, claims, actions, or proceedings of every kind and character . . . arising directly or indirectly from any activity . . . such as parachuting." In both cases, the negligence actions brought by students injured in parachute jumping were barred by the releases.

The RRO release is similar to those addressed in *Sommers* and *Cabel*. In the release Spencer signed, he specifically absolved [Rocky River Outfitters] RRO from liability for "any and all claims I have or may acquire against RRO for any personal injury or property damage I may sustain as a result of this rafting trip." Like the releases in *Sommers* and *Cabel*, this release specifically covered all claims that might arise from the specified activity in language that was obviously intended to be all-inclusive. **Because these cases are consistent with the plain-language principle underlying this state's cases, Spencer will probably not be able to recover from RRO for the injuries he has sustained.**

14
Drafting the Discussion

Changes From the Second Edition

We have expanded the discussion of the three major differences between undergraduate writing and legal writing and added some discussion of the use of introductory "roadmap" paragraphs. Some of the new appendixes in the teacher's manual supplement material in this chapter.

Teaching Notes

This chapter synthesizes the most important lessons of Parts B and C by showing students, step by step, how to put together a Discussion. For that reason, we try to teach this chapter before the first formal memo is due, even if we have to skip other chapters to do so. We return to those chapters later.

You might ask your students what changes they would make to the two discussions (the libel issue and the intent-to-publish sub-issue on pages 183-184 and the falsity sub-issue under Answer A on page 184) if they combined them. The question is worth discussing in class because it addresses the problem of overall organization and provides a nice transition to the exercises.

To combine the two discussions, at least two changes are necessary. First, the thesis paragraph for the libel issue needs to include a sentence or two concerning the falsity of the fliers. The revised paragraph is shown below, with new material:

Dooley did not commit libel. Libel is the "intentional publication of false statements about a person that humiliate that person or subject him to the loss of social prestige." *White v. Ball*. Two elements of this rule have been satisfied. The fliers were published when they were released by accident. The fliers also subjected Fremont to a loss of social prestige because they accused him of having a criminal record. Two elements require more discussion—the falsity of the flier and Dooley's intent. The fliers are false because Fremont has no criminal record. The intent element has not been met, however, because Dooley did not intend his fliers to be read by others.

Second, the discussion of the falsity sub-issue should go immediately after this paragraph, followed by the discussion of the intent sub-issue. Some teachers believe that the sub-issues that support your conclusion on an issue ought to be located before the sub-issues that support an opposing position. Under that approach, the intent sub-issue should be discussed before the falsity issue. Although this approach is acceptable, we believe that a good thesis paragraph *for a memorandum* generally provides sufficient guidance for the reader. As Chapter 21 (The Argument) states, however, briefs must be written differently.

Suggested Approach to Exercises

Exercise 14-A

This exercise gives students an opportunity to see the world from the teacher's point of view. That is, it asks them to read three discussions of the same issue, decide which they like the best, and explain why. In our experience, students like this type of exercise because it puts them in the position of praising and criticizing, rather than being praised and criticized. From a pedagogical point of view, the exercise reinforces the lessons of Chapter 14 by having students apply those lessons to someone else's writing.

One approach is to divide the class into groups of 3 or 4 and have each group grade one of the answers, using the grade criteria sheet in Appendix D. Then ask each panel to point out the strengths and weaknesses according to the criteria in this chapter. This approach gives the students valuable insight into how we assess the quality of their papers.

Another approach is to ask the class to evaluate the three answers according to the eight steps explained in the chapter. Before getting into details, you might ask students for their overall impressions—which they like better and why. Following is a commentary on the three answers.

Answer C is the best. The thesis paragraph explains the writer's conclusion on the overall issue in terms of the three elements and the facts of this case. It then states the rule in a way that makes the three elements clear.

The second paragraph begins with a topic sentence explaining the writer's conclusion on the first element (propensity toward violence), explains the law by synthesizing the two cases, and then explains how the law applies. It also answers a counterargument (violent hockey playing does not necessarily mean violence off the rink) by explaining that Deemer's behavior is violent even by hockey's standards.

The third and fourth paragraphs analyze the knowledge issue in two parts—actual knowledge (third paragraph) and constructive knowledge (fourth paragraph). The second element, of course, requires that the employer knew or should have known. The third paragraph also synthesizes the holdings of the two cases.

The next paragraph answers another counterargument (this case is different from the other two because Deemer had no criminal record for the employer to be aware of) by focusing the reader's attention on the rule itself (knowledge of propensity toward violence).

The last two paragraphs address the third element—the employer had the employee work in a place open to the public. The writer uses the analogous case and distinguishes *Hersh*. The discussion closes with a conclusion on the element and the overall issue. For this sub-issue, like the other two, a teacher can show how the writer addressed steps 2 through 7.

Answer A is the worst of the three. The thesis sentence does not incorporate the overall rule or the reasons for the writer's conclusion. The second sentence describes the *Tyus* case without first providing a topic sentence identifying the relevant sub-issue or the writer's conclusion.

The first five paragraphs contain a simultaneous discussion of two sub- issues—propensity toward violence and knowledge. You might use that to reinforce an important point from Chapters 6 (Identifying and Selecting Issues) and 10 (Organization): If students do not clearly separate elements, their discussion of sub-issues is likely to be confused.

The first and fourth paragraphs contain separate descriptions of the two cases. On both sub-issues, the writer could have synthesized the holdings and facts. Note the repetition this creates in the second and fifth paragraphs.

The discussion of the public place sub-issue in the last two paragraphs is the best part of Answer A, although it is not without problems.

Answer A contains other significant signposting and organizational problems. The fourth paragraph lacks a topic sentence, for example. The counterargument in the third paragraph comes before the writer has discussed the reasons for his conclusion on that point.

Answer A also contains several instances of vague editorializing that are not compatible with a precise analysis of the problem. The topic sentence of the last paragraph, for example, says the employer in the *Hersh* case "did the right thing." The next sentence explains what that means, but Answer A would be better if it did not include that phrase and continued directly into the next sentence. The comments about the Bolshoi ballet and "dangerous and frightening people like Deemer" add little to the analysis.

Finally, the conclusion is wrong. The issue is whether Watson is liable for assault, not whether he is liable for hiring Deemer. Also, if you want to explicitly anticipate Chapter 17 (The Discussion), you might point out that Answer A says Watson "is liable," a more certain conclusion than is warranted here. Answer C, by contrast, says Watson "is most likely responsible," a conclusion that is more objective than that in Answer A.

Answer B is better but still contains major problems. The thesis paragraph states a conclusion on each of the three elements and the facts of this case, and then describes the law as if it contained only two elements.

The second paragraph starts with a topic sentence on the "propensity" sub-issue but then describes the law on knowledge and applies that law to the facts of this case.

The third paragraph responds to a counterargument on the "propensity" sub-issue, which is confusing in this context. The topic sentence, which begins "Watson may argue that," is wordy and focuses attention on what Watson may argue rather than the position itself. The topic sentence in the fourth paragraph refers to "this conclusion," but it is not clear what "this" refers to.

The last two paragraphs address the public place sub-issue. The first few sentences of the last paragraph are wordy, however, and that paragraph repeats significant parts of the prior paragraph. The whole point of discussing your position first, of course, is to make the conclusion so clear that it does not need to be repeated.

Exercise 14-B

1.   Unlike most of these exercises, which involve several sub-issues, this problem involves only one issue—whether Dr. Farmer's negligence proximately caused Andrew Quale's death. For this reason, it may be a good introductory exercise for writing a discussion. This exercise can easily be resolved either way; some teachers may see it as a good writing exercise for that reason. The suggested approach below is based on a conclusion that Dr. Farmer is not liable.

Step 1 requires the student to state his or her overall conclusion about Dr. Farmer's liability and a brief explanation of the legal rules. Dr. Farmer is liable if (1) he was negligent and (2) his negligence proximately caused Andrew Quale's death. The student must explain that his negligence is a "given." Although the problem asks students to assume Dr. Farmer's negligence, the problem also states that Dr. Farmer did not examine the back of Andrew's head and did not use other standard diagnostic procedures. The student must also explain that the only issue is causation.

Step 2, which requires a topic sentence for this issue, is satisfied by a statement that Dr. Farmer's negligence did or did not proximately cause the boy's death. Students are likely to be divided on this issue. Note that students must follow Steps 2 through 7 for this issue even though those steps are written in terms of sub-issues. This principle is also explained on page 172.

Step 3 requires a description of the law. Answers here may vary a little, because the cases talk about both "a substantial possibility" and "more likely than not." The *Mallard* court treats them as interchangeable, and that is probably the best explanation. Students who use this explanation are more likely to conclude that Dr. Farmer is not liable, but others might rely on the expert's opinion that Andrew might have had a slightly greater than 50/50 chance of survival to reach the opposite conclusion. Students should also include the *Mallard* court's policy rationale that doctors should not be held liable for harm they "did not cause and may not have been able to prevent."

Step 4 requires an explanation of the analysis. Students who conclude that Dr. Farmer is not liable will most likely use *Mallard*. Like the decedent in *Mallard*, who had a possibility but not a probability of recovery with prompt surgery, Andrew Quale had an even chance, but not a probability, of recovery if Dr. Farmer had followed the proper procedures. Like the doctor in *Mallard*, Dr. Farmer should not be held liable for harm he did not cause and which he probably could not have prevented.

Step 5 requires a statement of the counterargument and its resolution. As noted above, students who conclude that Farmer is liable will argue that a better than 50/50 chance of survival is "substantial" under *Moulton* and consistent with the "more likely than not" language in *Mallard*. Step 6 requires a description of the law on which the counterargument would be based. Unless students have already explained *Moulton*, they would do so here. This explanation would include the facts, the holding, and the policy that certainty is not required. The counterargument would also be based on a strict reading of the "more likely than not" language in *Mallard*.

Step 7 requires an explanation. *Moulton* is distinguishable because the decedent in that case would have survived with surgery. Thus, even though the case talks about a substantial possibility, the facts involved a substantial certainty. Although the law does not require certainty in causation, it does require that the doctor's negligence more than likely caused the boy's death. Because that is not what happened here, Dr. Farmer is not liable.

Step 8 requires signposting. Here, students must evaluate their own writing in light of Chapter 13. Answers will vary, of course. Teachers might find this exercise a good one for peer review, for signposting as well as the other steps.

2.   This problem is exhaustively analyzed in this manual under Exercise 7-C. Also, there is an annotated sample discussion in Appendix B of this manual. The explanation here will therefore be in outline form.

The Step 1 thesis must state the student's conclusion on the overall issue of private nuisance and provide a brief explanation. It must describe the elements of the private nuisance rule, explain the two "givens" (Greenleaf's injury and Elliot's interference), and
identify the two sub-issues (legal right to free flow of light and unreasonableness of interference).

Steps 2 through 7 need to be repeated for each of these sub-issues. Students will often (though not always) find the interference to be unreasonable. That satisfies the Step 2 requirement for a statement of the student's conclusion on each sub-issue. The Step 3 description of the law will include the facts and holdings of the *Blum* and *Horton* cases. In Step 4, students will show how the facts of those cases are analogous to the facts of Greenleaf's case. The Step 5 counterargument might be based on a claim that the plaintiffs in the two cases were damaged more than Greenleaf. Students should state this counterargument and deny its validity in one or two sentences. (Note: There may be other counterarguments.) The legal basis for this counterargument under Step 6 might require some additional explanation of the facts of the cases, particularly concerning the relative amount of harm the plaintiffs suffered. In Step 7, students would explain that Greenleaf has been harmed in the same fundamental way as the melon grower in *Horton* and the farmer in *Blum*. Because Greenleaf's firm specializes in solar design, interference with the solar panels is equally fundamental and unreasonable to him.

For the sub-issue on the legal right to sunlight, the Step 2 statement of the student's conclusion should be that there is no legal right to the free flow of sunlight. Many of our students detest this conclusion, and many student papers will be written the other way. The Step 3 description of the law might include the legal rule from *Shover* and the facts, holding, and rationale in *Cassells*. The Step 4 explanation might show how *Cassells* is analogous to Greenleaf's case and would also explain that there is no case in this state holding that there is a legal right to the free flow of sunlight. Several counterarguments are possible for Step 5. One is that *Shover* is broad enough to include the free flow of light. Students who use this counterargument would include a sentence or two making this statement and denying its persuasiveness. Under Step 6, students might explain the facts and holding in *Shover*. Under Step 7, students would explain that the free flow of light and lateral support are different, and reiterate the lack of any judicial recognition of a free flow of light.

Students should then signpost the entire discussion under Step 8.

Exercise 14-C

1.   This is a good initial writing exercise because the analysis for one of the two sub-issues is already set out in Chapter 8. The only missing part of the analysis for the governmental functions sub-issue is a conclusion. If students have done Exercise 8-A, then this exercise mostly requires that students write what they have already analyzed.

The framework for this analysis should look something like the following. As noted earlier, although we reach certain conclusions about these sub-issues, you might just as easily reach other conclusions.

Step 1 (thesis on overall issue) needs to include the student's overall conclusion about whether the four Conservative members are a public body. On balance, we think a court would conclude that they are. This thesis should include the student's resolution of the "givens" (set out in the chart on page 94 of the text), and should also explain that "public body" is used both in the definition of "meeting" and in section 3. Finally, the thesis should identify the remaining sub-issues—whether the four members are a local legislative body and whether they are empowered to exercise governmental functions. This step should, in short, provide a framework for the discussion that follows.

Steps 2 through 7 must then be repeated for each sub-issue. If students have already done Exercise 8-A, they need only organize and write what they have already analyzed for the local legislative body sub-issue. Step 2 requires a statement of the writer's conclusion. We think a court would probably decide that the four Conservative members constitute a local legislative body. Step 3 requires a statement of the law—in this case, the relevant statutory language. Here it is essential to show the entire relevant text from section 2(b): "any state or local legislative body, including a board, commission, committee, subcommittee, authority, or council . . . ." Step 4 requires an explanation of the writer's conclusion. That the four members constitute, as a practical matter, a working budget committee is perhaps the best explanation. Students may also want to argue that the Conservatives are a council because they comprise a working majority of the Council.

Step 5 requires a statement of the counterargument and its resolution. In this case, we would say that it is irrelevant that the four members do not constitute a formal committee or subcommittee. Under Step 6, we would not repeat the statute but we would describe the *McPhee* case. Under Step 7, we would say that although the *McPhee* case applied to the entire board of education, its rationale that preliminary steps in the decision-making process should be public applies with equal force to meetings of committees or subcommittees. The statute does not require that the committee or subcommittee be "formal," in the sense of being appointed by the Council or in any other sense. Step 8 depends on what students write, but there should be at least three paragraphs, one for Step 1, one for the conclusion (Steps 2 through 4) on this sub-issue, and another for Steps 5 through 7 (the counterargument). The structure is unchanged even if students reach the opposite conclusion.

For the governmental functions sub-issue, Step 2 requires a statement of the conclusion. We would say that a court is likely to conclude that the four Conservative members are empowered to exercise governmental functions because they constitute a majority of the Council. Step 3 requires a description (preferably a quotation) of the relevant statutory language. Step 4 requires an explanation of the reasons. In this case, the fact that a majority can vote whatever budget it wants when the Council eventually meets, coupled with the *McPhee* court's explanation of the importance of subjecting preliminary meetings to public review, provides that explanation. Step 5 requires a statement of the counterargument. In this case, we would say that it is irrelevant that the four members do not constitute a quorum. We would skip Step 6 because there is no additional law to describe. Under Step 7, we would say that the four members can adopt whatever budget they want when the full Council meets, as it eventually must. Step 8 would depend on the way the discussion is written, but there should again be separate paragraphs for the discussion and the response to the counterargument.

2.   Begin with a conclusion stated in terms of the applicable law. For example, if the conclusion is that the League can probably intervene, the first sentence should say so and briefly say why. Then follow with a summary of the law. Students should quote the statute. If students have concluded that any of the requirements are "givens," they should explain those first. They may want to explain how a court is likely to resolve each sub-issue.

Steps 2 through 7 needs to be repeated for each sub-issue. Each sub-issue should begin with a conclusion, which should be stated in terms of the law applicable to that sub-issue.

These steps suggest answers to one of these sub-issues—timeliness. Thus:

> The League's application would be "timely" as required by the statute.

Following the conclusion on a sub-issue, describe the law. Here, the law will be the applicable part of the statute, which was already quoted in the thesis, followed by a discussion of that requirement's application in *Halsey*. For example:

> In *Halsey*, the court found that the plaintiffs' application was timely when it was filed only three weeks after the suit was filed. The court concluded there was no "unreasonable delay" in filing the application.

Note that this explanation includes the facts, the holding, and the court's reasoning.

Next, specifically explain how the law applies to the facts. Show how the facts are like or unlike those of *Halsey*. The student's analysis should be complete and explicit. For example:

> Similarly here, the League would file its application within a week or two after the city announced that it no longer represented the League's interest in this action. As in *Halsey*, there would be no unreasonable delay.

Although there is no explicit policy applicable in this example, be sure students include any policies or reasoning that explain how or why they think the law will be applied in a certain way.

After explaining how the law supports their position, they must turn to the counterargument:

> That the League's application would be filed more than six months after the original suit does not make it untimely.

Describe the law on which the counterargument would be based if it has not already been described. In the example used above, the counterargument would be based on *Halsey*, which has already been explained.

Finally, explain why the counterargument is unpersuasive. Reasoning and policy may also play a role in this step:

> The League believed the city would be representing its interests in the litigation until last week, when the city attorney said the city might be wrong. Because of this belief, the League did not intervene earlier. The timing of the League's application is therefore not unreasonable.

Students should follow Steps 2 through 7 for each of the three elements of the statute, as noted above. They should then pull together the various steps using the signposting materials in this chapter and in Chapter 13.

3.   Begin with a conclusion as to whether Odegaard has violated the statute and briefly explain why. Then summarize the applicable law. Here students would probably want to summarize section 31. Students should explain how all "givens" are resolved and identify sub-issues.

Steps 2 through 7 needs to be repeated for each sub-issue. Each sub-issue should begin with a conclusion, which should be an assertion that the law does or does not apply to the facts.

These steps suggest answers to one of these sub-issues—the "immediate family" exception.

> The court will likely conclude that Odegaard falls under the "immediate family" exception of section 31(c).

Following the conclusion on a sub-issue, describe the law. Here, the law will be the applicable part of the statute, followed by a discussion of the relevant case, *Toland*. In problems involving statutes, it is probably better to quote the relevant language at this step rather than in the thesis. For example:

> Section 31(b) exempts members of a candidate's "immediate family" from the $600 contribution limit in section 31(a). Subsection (c) defines "immediate family" as "a spouse, parent, brother, sister, son, or daughter." In *Toland v. Election Commission*, the court recognized that this exemption would ordinarily apply to direct contributions from a candidate's son. In declining to allow the son to be used as a conduit for contributions from non-family members, however, the court recognized that the Act's purpose of "reducing the corrupting influence of outside financial sources has much less force when the contributor is from the candidate's immediate family."

Next, specifically explain how the law applies to the facts. For example:

> Here, Rolf Odegaard is a parent to his granddaughter because he raised her from the time that she was very young. He is also her grandfather, not an unrelated adoptive parent. Applying the immediate family exemption to him is consistent with the statutory purpose of reducing the corrupting influence of outside money.

After explaining how the law supports their position, students must turn to the counterargument. In this case, there are two counterarguments to answer:

> Although the statute does not explicitly include grandparents in its definition, Odegaard's unique relationship with his granddaughter will likely convince

the court that the exemption should be applied here. The fact that he did not formally adopt her is unlikely to change this conclusion.

Describe the law on which the counterargument would be based if it has not already been done. In this example, the law has already been explained.

Finally, explain why the counterargument is unpersuasive. In this case, a detailed explanation would mostly repeat what has already been stated. Both counterarguments can be answered together and briefly:

> Odegaard's contribution is no more "corrupting" than would be a contribution from any other candidate's father.

Students should follow Steps 2 through 7 for the other sub-issue concerning the applicability of section 31(a), as noted above. They should then pull together the various steps using the signposting materials in this chapter and in Chapter 13.

15
Revising and Editing

Changes From the Second Edition.

There are no major changes from the second edition.

Teaching Notes

As noted at the beginning of Part C, this chapter lends itself to self-editing exercises and peer review. In addition to the exercises here, you may want to develop your own exercises from choice parts of student papers. We have pulled sentences or paragraphs from papers as we grade and have then handed them out as revising and editing exercises. You can emphasize certain writing problems by the sentences or paragraphs you chose.

Suggested Approach to Exercises

Exercise 15-A

There is more than one way to edit the following passages to remedy the problems of imprecision and wordiness. These are samples of the type of editing that is needed:

1. Note that in this passage the phrase "appearance of impropriety" has been retained even though it could be written without the nominalization. This phrase is a term of art used when discussing the application of Canon 9.

    > Canon 9 requires a lawyer to avoid even the appearance of impropriety. Although this requirement has led several courts to disqualify attorneys when no actual impropriety existed, the appearance of impropriety is not always sufficient to disqualify an attorney. For example, in *Blumenfeld v. Fusco*, the court held that the marriage of two attorneys employed by different firms did not create an appearance of impropriety sufficient to warrant disqualifying the wife. The case involved a challenge to a will, in which an associate in the firm representing the propounder was married to a partner in the firm retained to represent the caveator. The court found that no actual impropriety existed because the husband worked in the real estate department and had no contact with the attorneys who were actually representing the caveator. In declining to disqualify the wife, the court balanced the need to avoid the appearance of impropriety with the plaintiff's right to employ the counsel of his choice. The court concluded that the latter outweighed the former because any actual impropriety was unlikely.

2. This example contains some nominalizations that are awkward to replace with an adjective or verb. They have thus been left unchanged. Although the guidelines in this

chapter will generally improve the clarity of your students' writing, they are guidelines only and should not be applied mechanically.

No court has refused to consider fraud in an adoption case when there was evidence of active concealment. For example, *In re Baby J.*, the court found fraudulent concealment of the truth when the adoption agency told the parents that the birth mother was an eighteen-year-old unwed mother who could not care for the baby. In reality, the agency knew that the mother was a thirty-five-year-old patient in a mental institution and that the father was presumed to be another patient. The adoptive parents discovered the truth only after their thirteen-year-old adopted son was diagnosed as having an inherited mental disorder. Similarly, in *Roe*, the court awarded damages when the adoption agency placed three school-aged children for adoption, telling the prospective parents that the children were normal, healthy children. However, the agency had test results and psychological evaluations showing that the children had a history of dangerously violent behavior and other behavior disorders. In both cases, the court emphasized that the agencies knew and actively concealed the truth.

Exercise 15-B

Caution your students not to change the meaning of these sentences when editing. If the meaning of the sentence is not clear, they should decide what they think the writer was trying to say, and rewrite the sentence to express that thought more clearly. These sentences may be rewritten in a variety of ways. You may find it helpful to have the students work in groups to rewrite the sentences and then compare the results. Here are some examples of how the sentences may be rewritten:

1. Because medical malpractice lawsuits can be lengthy and expensive, plaintiffs and their attorneys should carefully weigh the chances of success before filing a complaint.

2. The defendant's fraudulent conduct was so reprehensible that the court should impose the maximum fine allowed.

3. The attorney strenuously objected to the witness' testimony as immaterial, irrelevant, and a product of hearsay.

4. In most jurisdictions, the "fireman's rule" bars any recovery by emergency personnel for injuries suffered in the line of duty.

5. Because the deadline for answering had passed, the attorney filed a motion to open the default.

6. The plaintiff alleged that the manufacturer's warning about the hazardous product was insufficient.

7.   Discrepancies in the defendant's testimony persuaded the jury of her guilt as to all charges.

8.   The plaintiff contended that he should be given a new trial because of the unethical conduct of the defendant's attorney.

9.   The court will hold the witness in contempt until he discloses the required information.

10.   The possible injury to the lake outweighs the benefits of a recreational camp.

Part D
The Office Memorandum

16
Elements of a Memorandum

Changes From the Second Edition

There are no major changes from the second edition.

Teaching Notes

The material in this chapter is best reinforced by a short lecture outlining the elements and pointing to the sample memorandum in Appendix A of the text. When you give your students a memorandum assignment, be sure to tell them whether you will require Brief Answers (which the text says are optional) or require them to write their memos in other ways that differ from the format described here. You should also tell your students whether you expect them to incorporate recommendations in the Conclusion.

You can use a memorandum assignment as a vehicle to revisit all of the basic concepts covered in Part B of the text. For example, the techniques in Chapter 5 (Understanding Legal Rules) and Chapter 6 (Identifying & Selecting Issues for Analysis) will help students develop the large-scale organization of their memo, while the techniques in Chapters 7 and 8 (Common Law Analysis and Statutory Analysis) can be used to begin to develop analogies and distinctions. The lessons in Part C will help students draft accurate descriptions of the law and clear explanations of their analysis of the issues and help them make their memo complete and reader-friendly.

The transition from writing discrete exercises to writing a complete legal document is an important one for students. Consider using this class to talk about professionalism and the role that writing will play in your students' careers. You might talk about the role that good writing and analysis will play on their law school exams. Some professors, looking beyond the first year, bring advertisements from the career development office to class, showing students that virtually all employers are looking for law clerks and associates who have strong research and writing skills. Learning legal writing and analysis is hard work; students benefit when we remind them what they are working _for_.

17
The Discussion

Changes From the Second Edition

There are no major changes from the second edition.

Teaching Notes

This chapter is for the office memorandum what Chapter 21 (The Argument) is for briefs. This chapter discusses objectivity in memorandum writing, and Chapter 21 discusses advocacy in brief writing.

Chapter 17 gives you another opportunity to refer back to earlier chapters as students apply some of the fundamental skills they have already learned in the context of a formal memorandum. Chapters 10 (Organization) and 14 (Drafting the Discussion) are particularly relevant, and some teachers work with all three of these chapters at the same time, showing students how the essential principles of good organization remain constant.

Suggested Approach to Exercises

Exercise 17-A

If students have already worked through Exercise 10-A, this exercise requires them to draft a Discussion from their outline response to Question 5 in that exercise. If they have not, the Discussion should be based on the kind of analysis shown in the suggested response to Exercise 10-A, Question 5, in this manual. This exercise works well as a hand-in assignment or as an exercise students share with their classmates for peer review.

The answer we outlined for that exercise provides a starting point. The students should follow the Chapter 14 steps for translating their outlines into a Discussion. In the context of this chapter, you might consider these teaching points:

- ► Objectivity in drawing a conclusion. Problems to look for include waffling, overconfidence, advocacy, and underconfidence.

- ► Objectivity in describing the law. Problems to look for include failure to explain the elements (particularly the confidential relationship element in *Kendall*) and selective use of facts from the cases.

- ► Objectivity in explaining the analysis. Problems to look for include failure to discuss counterarguments, failure to consider relevant facts, advocacy, and failure or reluctance to acknowledge the strength of particular conclusions.

Exercise 17-B

If students have already worked through Exercise 10-B, this exercise requires them to draft a Discussion from their outline response to question 5 in that exercise. If they have not, the Discussion should be based on the kind of analysis shown in the suggested response to Exercise 10-B, Question 5, in this manual. This exercise works well as a hand-in assignment or as an exercise students share with their classmates for peer review.

The answer we outlined for that exercise provides a starting point. The students should follow the Chapter 14 steps for translating their outlines into a Discussion. In the context of this chapter, you might consider these teaching points, which are virtually identical to those for Exercise 17-A:

▶ Objectivity in drawing a conclusion. Problems to look for include waffling, overconfidence, advocacy, and underconfidence. These points are particularly important for the issues raised by this problem, because students may follow their feelings.

▶ Objectivity in describing the law. Problems to look for include failure to explain the elements (particularly the unreasonable interference element in *Peters*) and selective use of facts from the cases.

▶ Objectivity in explaining the analysis. Problems to look for include failure to discuss counterarguments, failure to consider relevant facts, advocacy, and failure or reluctance to acknowledge the strength of particular conclusions.

18
Statement of Facts for a Memorandum

Changes From the Second Edition

We changed the dates in the example.

Teaching Notes

Many students have trouble writing objectively, especially when they know which of the parties in a problem is "their" client. To help them understand what an objective statement of facts should look like, consider dividing your class into three groups: plaintiffs, defendants, and law clerks or judges. Give each group a sufficient amount of time to write an objective statement of facts for Exercise 18-A, then compare the results and discuss their differences.

Some first-year law students also have trouble writing fact statements because they lack confidence in their ability to identify the legally significant facts in a problem. Consequently, they err on the side of including information lest they inadvertently omit something important, they are easily distracted by emotional facts that "feel" important but in fact are not, or they miss the undramatic but essential fact. Both exercises below give you an opportunity to explore these common problems with your students.

Suggested Approach to Exercises

Exercise 18-A

1.   Legally significant facts are those that affect whether the property was fit for human habitation. These facts include:

> ►   Farley leased the apartment.
> ►   The toilet did not work.
> ►   There was no hot water.
> ►   There were two rats in the apartment.
> ►   Cockroaches were everywhere.
> ►   Some walls had large holes.
> ►   The floors and walls were grimy.
> ►   Several windows were broken.
> ►   The rental agent refused to rescind the lease.

These facts all concern the habitability of the apartment itself. Some students will want to say that conditions outside the apartment are also relevant to its habitability, and you might ask them to explain why. (In fact, you might respond to every assertion that a certain fact is legally significant by asking why.) Those facts are:

> Two vagrants were asleep on the front steps.
> The hubcaps on Farley's car were stolen while he was in the apartment.

Students might think that some facts are legally significant when they are not. For example, the representations about the apartment in the ad and by the rental agent are not legally significant because the warranty of habitability is implied from the leasing of the property. These facts, however, have considerable emotional importance.

2. It probably matters that Farley's hubcaps were stolen. Some students will argue that this is relevant to the warranty of habitability. You can use this question to emphasize the cumulative effect of the facts about the habitability of the apartment. If you remove one of those facts, does the outcome change? Two of the facts? Most of the time, the answer will be no. You can also use this question to show that some of the facts are more important than others, even facts about the habitability of the apartment. Thus, while it probably matters that the hubcaps were stolen, it does not matter much because the claim does not hinge on any one fact.

3. Basic background facts: Farley had just moved to the city, was looking for an apartment, answered a newspaper ad, and leased the apartment before he looked at it based on the agent's representations, and then discovered the condition of the apartment. These facts, which can be explained in a little more detail, tell the story and provide a context for this problem.

4. The Statement of Facts might begin with some of the background facts described in Answer 3 above. That is, Farley moved to the city, was looking for an apartment, answered a newspaper ad, and leased an apartment based on the rental agent's representations before he looked at it. The factual statement would then include a detailed description of what he saw when he visited the apartment. It would conclude with a statement that the agent refused to rescind the lease.

Exercise 18-B

1. For teachers who use Exercise 10-B, this is a good place to emphasize another use of the charts described in Chapters 6, 7, and 8. The significant facts of this case should be those identified in those charts. In this case, the significant facts are drawn from the elements charts used to help answer Exercise 10-B:

Regulation issue:
> Powerhouse has capacity of 500,000 pounds of steam per hour.
> Powerhouse burns coal containing 0.9% to 1.2% sulfur by weight.

Nuisance issue:
> All-Rite owns land on which the factory is located or a leasehold estate in the land.
> The factory emits sulfur dioxide into the air.
> All-Rite employs 490 people and provides much income for the community.

► Coal has lower sulfur content than coal burned in other states.
► Sulfur dioxide emissions reduce value of farmers' crops by 5%, reduce value of their property by $5,000 to $10,000, and probably increase their respiratory ailments.
► These crops are grown on the farmers' land.

Trespass issue (facts not already listed):
► Sulfur dioxide settles on farmers' alfalfa fields.
► It may be economically feasible for All-Rite to further control emissions.
► All-Rite's sulfur dioxide emissions are from a short smokestack.
► All-Rite's emissions are not necessary to save human life or health.

2. Key background facts might include:

►   All-Rite factory makes chemicals, inks, and dyes for many commercial products.
►   Source of information about damages (e.g., tax assessor, physician), and details about alfalfa damage (e.g., whitens leaves).
►   All-Rite has ignored the farmers' complaints.

Students may want to include the newspaper's advocacy on behalf of the company, but these additional facts are not legally or (for the most part) emotionally significant.

3. Students may find this problem a bit challenging because the statement does not lend itself to a chronological account. The third principle in the chapter (Organize the facts intelligibly) provides a useful starting point, however. The statement is more intelligible if the facts concerning the factory's operations and emissions are described before the farmer's complaints, for example, because the complaints make no sense otherwise.

Because of the use of charts in identifying facts, moreover, students may be tempted to organize the statement according to issues and sub-issues. Students may need to be reminded that they must tell a story. For example, each of the three legal rules involves facts concerning the plant's emissions. Students should, of course, group those facts rather than state them in three separate places.

The fourth principle (Describe the facts accurately and objectively) will be a problem for some students because they will characterize the facts or generalize about them. This may occur because students have strong feelings about what the outcome should be or because they are not thinking precisely.

19
Questions Presented

Changes From the Second Edition

We increased the dollar amounts in Exercise 19-A.

Teaching Notes

The handout in Appendix E of this manual summarizes one process to use when writing Questions Presented and offers additional examples. The first example is based on Exercise 14-A. The second is based on a problem that is not in the book. It should serve as an example of questions that are understandable to a reader unfamiliar with the law and facts of a problem. Note that the second example is set in the fictional state of East Dakota. You may want to change that to a real state that has a similar parental liability statute.

Suggested Approach to Exercises

Exercise 19-A

1.   For in-class discussion, this question might best be answered with elements charts.

The first issue is whether the contract complies with the statute of frauds. The statute requires that a contract (1) for the sale of land or a legal interest in land (2) must be in writing and (3) must be signed by the persons to be charged with the contract. In the *Treacher* case, the court interpreted the second element to require that the writing identify with reasonable certainty and accuracy (a) the parties to the contract, (b) the subject matter to which the contract relates, and (c) the terms and conditions of all promises, including payment conditions. Students can eliminate several "givens" from detailed discussion. This contract was for the sale of land or a legal interest in land. The napkin stated the parties to the contract and the subject matter. Thus, the issue involves two sub-issues:

(1)   Whether the contract complies with the statute of frauds.
   a.   Whether the contract states with reasonable certainty and accuracy the terms and conditions of all promises.
   b.   Whether the contract was signed by the persons to be charged.

The second issue is whether the contract is unenforceable based on fraud. As the *Divine* case indicates, there are six elements: (1) false representations, (2) of material facts, (3) that the defendant knew were false, (4) that the defendant intended the plaintiff to rely on, (5) that the plaintiff was justified in relying on, and (6) the plaintiff suffered damages as a result of this reliance. Again, many of these are "givens." Zoeller's representations were false, and they concerned material facts that Zoeller knew were false. Zoeller also intended that Hughes rely on these facts. The other two are harder.

Thus, this issue also involves two sub-issues:

(2)   Whether the contract is unenforceable based on fraud.
        a. Whether Hughes was justified in relying on Zoeller's representations.
        b. Whether Hughes suffered damage as a result of her reliance.

2.   Legally significant facts include the following:

(1)   Whether the contract complies with the statute of frauds.
        a.   Whether the contract states with reasonable certainty and accuracy the terms and conditions of all promises.
                ► Napkin describes property as Blue Goose Inn
                ► Napkin states purchase price.
                ► Napkin does not state payment conditions.
        b.   Whether the contract was signed by the persons to be charged.
                ► Zoeller wrote the offer.
                ► Hughes did not accept in writing.
                ► She orally agreed, and her oral agreement was recorded on a tape recorder.
(2)   Whether the contract is unenforceable based on fraud.
        a.   Whether Hughes was justified in relying on Zoeller's representations.
                ► Zoeller showed Hughes altered books and falsely represented the property's value to her.
                ► Zoeller held himself out as a good businessman.
                ► Hughes knew the books were altered.
                ► Hughes was drinking while Zoeller made these representations and intoxicated when she said she accepted.
        b.   Whether Hughes suffered damage as a result of her reliance.
                ► Sale price exceeds market value of the property by $40,000.
                ► Tavern has made a profit of $25,000 for the last three years, and profits may double or triple in the near future.

3.   As the structure of the answer to Question 2 indicates, the last step is pretty straightforward if students use this process. Students may have trouble with at least two things. Some students will have difficulty with Questions Presented when there are issues and sub-issues. The first Question Presented in the memo in Appendix A suggests a solution. Some students will also have difficulty framing a question when there are many facts. The reasonableness of Hughes' reliance, for example, involves more facts than students can probably put in a single question. Encourage them to be concise and choose only the most important facts.

Example:

I.   Whether a contract for the sale of a tavern complies with the statute of frauds.

       A.   Whether the contract states with reasonable certainty and accuracy the terms and conditions of all promises when it included only the name of the tavern and purchase price and not the conditions of payment.

       B   .Whether the contract was signed by the person to be charged when the seller wrote the contract on a napkin, the buyer did not accept in writing but she orally agreed to the contract, and her agreement was recorded on tape.

II.   Whether the contract was procured by fraud and is therefore enforceable.

       A.   Whether the buyer was justified in relying on the seller's representations when he falsely represented the value of the property and showed the buyer business records that had been altered, the buyer knew the records had been altered, and the buyer was intoxicated when she accepted the offer.

       B.   If so, whether the buyer has suffered damaged as a result of her reliance when the sale price exceeded the market value of the property by $40,000 but the tavern had made a profit of $25,000 each year for the last three years and profits may double or triple in the near future.

Exercise 19-B

1.   If students have already completed Exercise 10-B, this question is not necessary. The process for identifying relevant rules, elements, issues, and sub-issues for this problem is shown in the answer to that exercise. The answer to Exercise 10-B showed the following issues and sub-issues:

      (1)   Whether All-Rite's interference with the use and enjoyment of the farmers' property is unreasonable and therefore a nuisance.

      (2)   Whether All-Rite's sulfur dioxide emissions trespass on the farmers' land.
         a.   Whether the sulfur dioxide emissions are tangible and therefore physically invade the farmers' land.
         b.   Whether All-Rite's emissions are privileged by necessity.

2.   The legally significant facts for each issue and sub-issue, which are drawn from the charts used to answer Exercises10-B and 18-B, include the following:

      (1)   All-Rite employs 490 people and provides much income for the community. The coal has lower sulfur content than coal burned in other states. Sulfur dioxide emissions reduce the value of the farmers' crops by 5%, reduce the value of their property by $5,000 to $10,000, and probably increase their respiratory ailments.

These crops are grown on the farmers' land. All-Rite may be able to do more to reduce emissions.

    (2)   a.   Sulfur dioxide is emitted into the air and settles on the farmers' alfalfa fields.

                b.   All-Rite employs 490 people, but it may be economically feasible for All-Rite to further control emissions. All-Rite's emissions are not necessary to save human life or health.

3.   This question requires only that the students assemble the relevant parts of each of the previous questions into Questions Presented.

      The hardest Question Presented to draft is likely to be the one concerning nuisance because of the numerous facts. You may want to discuss the various facts and try to identify those that are most important. The facts concerning damage are important, for example, but do each of these facts have equal value?

Additional Exercise

Exercise 19-C

Identify the relevant rules, issues, and significant facts in Exercise 11-C and draft the Questions Presented.

Suggested Approach   This exercise presents a challenge because the issue is composed of alternatives rather than elements or factors. The broad question is who owns the trees. The answer depends on how the trees are characterized. They are real property or personal property, and personal property only if they are crops or stock in trade. This exercise might work best as a class exercise rather than as a take-home assignment.

      Here is an example of how the questions could be drafted. Because all of the significant facts are relevant to each sub-issue, they are grouped together in the main question:

Whether young trees planted in the backyard of residential property belong to the purchasers of the property or to the previous owners of the property when the previous owner purchased the trees for resale in their nursery, temporarily planted the trees in the yard because there was no space in the nursery, and did not remove them prior to selling the property.

A.   Whether the trees belong to the purchasers of the property according to the common law rule that plants growing in the soil are part of the real estate.

B.   Whether the trees belong to the sellers because they are either
      1.   crops, which are defined as plants placed in the soil that the owner intends to harvest and which are the personal property of the owner who planted them, or
      2.   stock in trade, which is defined as goods or chattel obtained by a merchant for the purpose of resale and which are the personal property of the merchant.

Part E
Briefs

20
Elements of a Brief

Changes From the Second Edition

The examples under Parts 4 (Opinions Below) and 5 (Jurisdiction) have been updated.

Teaching Notes

As with the elements of a memorandum, the elements of a brief are perhaps best introduced with a short lecture. There are at least two ways to teach the elements of a brief. The first is based on the elements contained in this chapter. The second is based on the relevant court rules in a particular jurisdiction. Many court rules specifically identify the elements of a brief and the order in which those elements must appear. The first approach is simple and straightforward. An advantage of the second approach is that it prepares students for what they will have to do in practice.

Some teachers find it helpful, when introducing briefs, to list the elements of a memo on the board alongside the elements of a brief, and then compare and contrast individual elements in each column. This works particularly well with trial court briefs.

Appendixes B, C, E, and F in the text are very helpful in teaching the elements of a brief. First, they show entire briefs to trial and appellate courts using the format described in this chapter. Second, they show how opposing sides might handle each element and thus provide a basis for more detailed study of individual elements. This is particularly helpful for elements for which there is no detailed explanation in other chapters (*e.g.*, Questions Presented, Standard of Review).

Some professors have used the following technique to demonstrate the principles discussed in this part of the text. Your students are probably working on a persuasive writing project of some kind while you are teaching these chapters, often a trial brief and then an appellate brief. Regardless of the writing assignment that your students are doing, consider obtaining copies of the briefs filed by the parties in one of the cases that your students are using for their assignment. If, for example, they are working on an assignment involving a defendant's *Miranda*[9] rights, obtain copies of the principal briefs in the case and select examples from each one for comparison. Study the examples from the case as you reach each new chapter in the text. For example, compare the parties' argument on a certain point in connection with Chapter 21 (The Argument) and analyze their handling of a key case, compare the point headings for that issue when you reach Chapter 22 (Point Headings), or consider the differences between the parties' description of a particular incident when you reach Chapter 23 (Statement of Facts for a Brief). By using a familiar case that is relevant to their assignment, you can show students how the principles described in the text are actually used—or perhaps not used—in a context that is immediately relevant to their own work

---

[9] *Miranda v. Arizona*, 384 U.S. 436 (1966).

21
The Argument

Changes From the Second Edition

Part 6 (Maintain a Professional Tone) is new. Exercise 21-C has been updated.

Teaching Notes

Exercises 21-A and 21-B involve very similar facts and law. If you need a simple exercise, Exercise 21-A will suit your needs. If you want a more challenging exercise, Exercise 21-B is a better choice. Most teachers chose one exercise or the other, depending on their needs. If you have more time, however, Exercises 21-A and 21-B can be taught in sequence. The following notes will help you decide how to use these exercises.

Exercise 21-A is a good starting point for constructing arguments as to why the law supports your position. The issue is easy to formulate: Do Jones's actions fit within the judicially created exception to the statute? Exercise 21-B is more complicated because it requires students to progress from the broad issue to narrower issues, as illustrated by the inverted pyramid below.

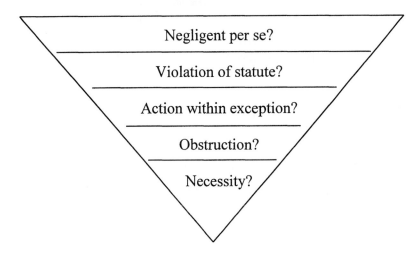

Exercise 21-B thus presents more of a challenge regarding how to present the law and the facts most favorably for your client. Taken together, the two exercises illustrate how the nature of the relevant law often dictates how you organize and present your arguments.

If you use both exercises, encourage your students to identify the specific question posed by each exercise. Notwithstanding the similar law and facts, the question in 21-A is not whether Jones violated the statute but whether the exception applies. In 21-B, however, the question is whether Hardy violated the statute.

Suggested Approach to Exercises

Exercise 21-A

This exercise works extremely well in classroom discussion as an introduction to advocacy. Some of us outline the argument for each side on the chalkboard as we go through class, so that students can see the competing arguments side by side at the end.

This exercise also works well as an exercise in synthesizing cases. Basically, each side is obliged to interpret the cases in a way that supports its position. Although the statutory rule contains no exceptions, and the earliest (*Cain*) case said there could be no exceptions, the court of appeals has created an exception. The problem involves a choice of law (the rule or the exception) and a question of how the exception should be defined.

You might ask the following questions to develop each side's argument: Will your side rely on the exception or the rule? What is the legal basis for the exception/rule? How would you say that law applies here? What counterargument will your opponent make? What law will your opponent rely on? What is the source of that law? What is your answer? At the end, you might get something like this:

Jones	State
The charge should be dismissed. The public necessity exception (*McKinney, Gordon dicta*) applies here because Jones avoided a potentially serious accident with his fuel truck when he swerved to avoid hitting an unexpected ice patch.	The charge should not be dismissed. Statute specifically requires drivers to keep their trucks in the right lane. *Gordon* and rationale in *Cain* are applicable.
Because this was a real emergency, *Gordon* is inapplicable.	
This is not about financial self-interest, and *Shoop* is thus not applicable.	Jones swerved into left lane because he was trying to protect valuable fuel, and thus *Shoop* applies.
Cain does not apply because the law has changed.	There was no emergency here because Jones should have been watching for ice patches. *McKinney* and *Gordon dicta* do not apply.

Notice the marginal value of *Cain*, even to the state. Although it said there could be no exceptions, the court has subsequently created exceptions.

This problem can also be approached in more complicated ways. One teacher, for example, creates vertical columns for each of the four cases as well as this case. On the left side of this chart, the teacher writes these factors: danger without lane change, danger with lane change, type of maneuver, whether the condition was expected or not, whether actual harm occurred, and whether the defendant's conviction was upheld. Each case is then analyzed for these factors. The teacher uses this approach to get a clear understanding of which cases provide the strongest basis for each side's position, although the result is about the same as that described above.

Exercise 21-B

1.   **(a)**   Tri-State's counsel would emphasize the exception. Hardy violated the general rule by driving on the left side of the road, but Tri-State will argue that she fits within the exception because an obstruction made it necessary for her to swerve into the left lane.

(b)   Tri-State's actions fell within the statutory provision that drivers may drive in the left lane to avoid an obstruction because pumpkins falling from a truck immediately ahead of Tri-State's driver created an obstruction.

(c)   (1)   The pumpkins were an obstruction. There were at least eleven of them, each weighing from fifteen to twenty pounds, and they fell off a truck immediately ahead of the Tri-State truck.

(2)   The obstruction made it necessary to swerve into the left lane. Hitting the pumpkins may have caused the fuel tanker truck to go out of control, crash, and explode. There was a sharp embankment on the right side. Thus, going into the left lane was the only reasonable alternative to endangering the lives of both drivers.

[Note that the arguments track the relevant statutory language: (1) an obstruction (2) making it necessary.]

(d)   (1)   The pumpkins were an obstruction. *James* illustrates that an obstruction can be anything making it dangerous to continue in the right lane. *Yerrick* is distinguishable because there was no obstruction precluding safe passage, merely a bumpy and uneven stretch of road.

(2)   The obstruction made it necessary to swerve into the left lane. In *James* the court refused to interpret the statute so strictly as to force the driver to choose between hitting a child and subjecting himself to a negligence suit by driving on the left side of the road. The Tri-State driver faced a similar choice. In both cases, the drivers were concerned with saving lives. By contrast, the driver in *Yerrick* was concerned only with possible damage to his car.

(e)   To show obstruction:
  ▶ Size of pumpkins and that they are slippery when squashed

[Some students will say that the pumpkins were an obstruction or created a hazard. Point out that these are conclusions, not facts.]

To show necessity:

> ➤   Suddenness of latch opening and pumpkins falling out
> ➤   Highly flammable oil in Tri-State truck
> ➤   Experienced driver
> ➤   Sharp drop on right side and extremely narrow shoulder
> ➤   Unaware of oncoming car

(f)   The policy implicit in *James* is that one should try to protect lives by choosing the least dangerous alternative.

(g)   The counterargument will be that there was no obstruction because several cars ran over the pumpkins without incident. The refutation is that the pumpkins may have presented an obstruction to trucks but not to cars. [Several years ago, one of us had a legal writing student who had driven trucks for several years. He told the class that he would *never* drive over pumpkins that large if he could avoid it, because of the danger of the truck skidding out of control.] Also, the Tri-State driver had to make an immediate decision because the pumpkins spilled out suddenly. As an experienced driver, she was in the best position to know what action she should take to avoid possible loss of life. [That she had to make an immediate decision and did not see Hansen's car also helps to refute the argument that driving into the left lane and possibly hitting another vehicle was a more dangerous course of action than hitting the pumpkins.]

(h)   Students should draft the argument based on answers to the previous questions. You might have students exchange their answers with students representing Hansen.

2.   **(a)**   Hansen's counsel will emphasize the general rule to show that Tri-State's driver was negligent *per se.*

    (b)   Tri-State was negligent *per se* because its driver violated section 98.01 by driving a truck in the left lane when there was no obstruction in the right lane, only some pumpkins which several cars subsequently ran over without incident.

    (c)   (1)   Because Tri-State's driver crossed into the left lane, the company violated the statute and was negligent *per se.*

                  (2)   The pumpkins were not an obstruction. Some smashed upon impact. Several cars hit unbroken pumpkins and continued moving forward.

                  (3)   Swerving into the left lane was not necessary. Even if the pumpkins were considered an obstruction so that it was dangerous to drive over them, the truck driver created a greater danger by moving into the path of oncoming traffic.

    (d)   (1)   Because Tri-State's driver crossed into the left lane, the company violated the statute and was negligent *per se. Meekhof* applied the general rule and

138

stated its purpose of protecting persons and property on the left side of the road.

(2) The pumpkins were not an obstruction. This case is similar to *Yerrick*, where the obstruction was bumps and unevenness in the road. As in *Yerrick*, the driver could have continued forward with some possible damage to the truck but with little risk of loss of life. *James* is distinguishable because the "obstruction" in that case was a child.

(3) Swerving into the left lane was not necessary. As in *Meekhof* (driver intoxicated) and *Yerrick* (driver seeking to avoid bumps in the road), it was not necessary for the Tri-State driver to swerve into the left lane. This case presents a situation the exact opposite of that in *James*. In *James*, the driver swerved to avoid killing a person directly in front of the truck. In this case, Tri-State's driver swerved to avoid pumpkins and took a chance of killing or seriously injuring a motorist traveling in the proper lane.

(e) To show no obstruction:
  - ► Only eleven pumpkins recovered; others smashed on impact
  - ► Cars hit pumpkins and did not go out of control
  - ► Tri-State's truck was large and heavy

To show no necessity:
  - ► Experienced driver (could have controlled truck)
  - ► Pickup driver pulled over onto shoulder (implying Tri-State driver could have done the same)

To show policy of protecting persons on left side of road:
  - ► Hansen severely injured

(f) The purpose of the statute is to protect persons and property on the left side of the road. *Yerrick*; *Meekhof*. If the pumpkins in this case are considered an obstruction, the rule will be swallowed up with similar exceptions and the legislative purpose will be avoided.

(g) The Tri-State driver had a cargo of highly flammable fuel and had to make an immediate decision about three dangerous alternatives: (1) to continue on the right side of the roadway, run over the pumpkins, and risk losing control of the truck, with the possibility that the truck would crash and explode; (2) to pull over to the right side and risk falling down the embankment; (3) to swerve to the left and risk colliding with another vehicle. She chose the alternative with the least chance of endangering lives. The refutation is that because the pumpkins were not an obstruction that prevented safe passage, Tri-State's driver misjudged the situation and made an ill-considered choice. She should have continued on the right side of the road and avoided endangering persons properly traveling in the left lane (the class of persons the statute is designed to protect).

[Some students make assumptions—for example, that Hardy was following too closely—and then state them as facts. This gives you an opportunity to explain the difference between facts reasonably inferred from those given and mere speculation. You might also ask students what facts missing from this exercise they would try to discover in a real case. For example: How closely was Hardy following the pickup truck? If she was following from a safe distance, could she have avoided the pumpkins by stopping? Were there vehicles behind her that would have been endangered by her sudden stop?]

(h)   Students should draft the argument based on their answers to the previous questions. You might have students exchange their answers with students representing Tri-State.

The chart on the following page summarizes the arguments for each side.

Tri-State	Hansen
Thesis: Hardy's actions fell within the statutory provision that drivers may drive in the left lane when necessary to avoid an obstruction.	**Thesis:** Hardy violated the statute and thus was negligent per se.
Language of statute	**Language of statute**
Obstruction > 15-20 lb. pumpkins fell from truck immediately ahead of Hardy > pumpkins are slippery when squashed > thus, they are an obstruction to trucks though not necessarily to cars, several of which ran over the pumpkins > similar to James, where driver swerved because of danger to child if he continued in the right lane > different from Yerrick, where there was no obstruction, only a bumpy and uneven road	No obstruction > some pumpkins smashed on impact > several cars ran over pumpkins without incident > similar to Yerrick, where there was only a bumpy road > different from James, where there was an actual "obstruction," a child > policy: if pumpkins are considered an obstruction in this case, the rule would be swallowed up with exceptions
Necessity > suddenness of latch opening created situation where Hardy had to make an instant decision > flammable oil in truck could explode if Hardy lost control of truck > policy: implicit in James, where driver swerved to avoid hitting a child, is that a driver should choose the least dangerous alternative–the policy behind the exception in the statute > sharp drop on right created danger of truck falling down embankment > experienced driver unaware of oncoming car– made the best decision under the circumstances	**No necessity** > even if pumpkins an obstruction, Hardy created a greater danger by swerving–truck more likely to explode from hitting another vehicle than by running over pumpkins > unlike situation in James, where driver swerved to avoid hitting a child, Hardy swerved and thus endangered motorist driving in the proper lane > as an experienced driver, should have been able to control the truck and handle the situation properly > swerving to avoid pumpkins is similar to the situations in Yerrick (driver seeking to avoid damage to car) where there was no necessity > policy: purpose of statute is to protect drivers on the left side of the lane
Conclusion: compliance with statute, so not negligent per se	**Conclusion**: violation of statute, so negligence per se

Exercise 21-C

The factual and legal materials for this problem are also used in Exercises 22-B and 23-B.

1.   The issues are (1) whether the state will continue to recognize parental immunity, and (2) if not, whether it will adopt the exceptions for parental supervision and care adopted in *Geller* or the reasonable parent rule adopted in *Peterson*.

2.   **(a/b)**   The Lees' strongest and most significant issue is whether the state will apply parental immunity in this case. It is the strongest because binding precedent, *Lanir v. Lanir*, favors their position. It is the most significant because if it is resolved in their favor, they win without regard to whether they fall within the *Geller* or *Peterson* rules.

         (c)   Outline of Lees' arguments, the counterarguments, and the responses:

               (1)   <u>Position</u>: The doctrine of parental immunity precludes PlayChem's defense that the parents were contributorily negligent.

                     <u>Reasons</u>: The doctrine is the law of the state. The Supreme Court adopted the doctrine of parental immunity in *Lanir v. Lanir* when it refused to allow a child to sue his father.

                     <u>Counterargument</u>: *Lanir* is not controlling because it did not explicitly adopt parental immunity in all cases and inapposite because it did not concern a suit between the child's parents and a third party.

                     <u>Response</u>: This case is within the rule as well as the reasoning of *Lanir*. The *Lanir* court believed that parent and child should not be on opposite sides of a lawsuit. A similar situation will occur if PlayChem is allowed to assert the parents' negligence as a bar to the child's recovery.

               (2)   <u>Position</u>: The parental immunity doctrine serves important public policies.

                     <u>Reasons</u>: It fosters harmony within the family unit by precluding a child from suing her parents and prevents the family's financial resources from being depleted by intra-family suits. Neither policy would be served if the contributory negligence defense pits the parents against the child. Family harmony would be disrupted and the family's resources would be diminished by barring the child's recovery for the negligence of a third party. Parental immunity also reduces the incidence of collusive lawsuits.

Counterargument: One traditional reason for the parental immunity doctrine, that it depletes the family coffers, no longer applies. An insurance company, not by the individual, usually pays damages for torts. Another traditional reason, that it fosters family harmony, was never sound to begin with. The law does not prohibit lawsuits between parents and children over property disputes, yet these kinds of disputes are more likely to occur than lawsuits in tort. Similar reasoning applies to the danger of collusive lawsuits: Any kind of lawsuit could be collusive.

Response: The traditional reasons for parental immunity are particularly applicable in this case. If the contributory negligence defense is allowed, the child will not be recompensed for her injuries, and the family resources will be depleted accordingly. This circumstance would be due to the contributory negligence of her parents, a fact which will tend to destroy rather than promote family harmony. This case also illustrates the danger of collusion, in theory if not in fact.

(3)   Position: The court should not adopt the *Geller* exception nor replace the doctrine with a "reasonable parent" rule (*Peterson)*.

[The arguments and counterarguments on this point are outlined in the answer to 3(c).]

(4)   Position: If the court does adopt the *Geller* rule, the Lees are still immune.

Reason: This case does not concern either of the two *Geller* exemptions. Because use of the chemistry set was not part of the state's required education, it is outside the *Geller* exemptions.

Counterargument: The use of the chemistry set was part of an educational program the parents voluntarily designed for Susan. This program was part of "the provision of food, clothing, housing, medical care, and other care" under the second *Geller* exemption.

Response: The chemistry set had no connection to the university program where Susan was voluntarily enrolled. In addition, the second *Geller* exemption applies only when the parents are performing a legal obligation.

[This outline does not contain an argument like (4) for the *Peterson* rule. If the court adopts the *Peterson* rule, the Lees may be liable. Thus, the Lees' only argument about the *Peterson* rule is that the court should not adopt it (3).]

(d) Students should draft the argument based on the outline used to answer 2(c). You might have students exchange their arguments with students representing PlayChem.

2. **(a/b)** PlayChem's strongest issue is whether the Lees fall within a recognized exception to parental immunity. It is strongest because PlayChem has a better chance of convincing the court to reach a limited decision holding parents liable in some situations than to abolish parental immunity altogether. The most significant issue is whether the state should abolish parental immunity. If PlayChem wins this argument, it will not have to undergo another trial to determine its negligence. If PlayChem wins judicial recognition of a limited exception to parental immunity, however, it will have to undergo another trial.

(c) Outline of PlayChem's arguments, the counterarguments, and the responses:

[The PlayChem defense raises issues of strategy and organization. The PlayChem advocate would have to decide whether to argue for the abolition of parental immunity, an argument it is likely to lose. We decided to make the abolition argument, but to place it last even though it is the most significant. The argument will appear stronger after the court has considered the other alternative arguments.]

    (1) <u>Position</u>: The court should adopt an exception to the parental immunity doctrine that parents are immune only when they are negligent in providing to their child the supervision and care which they are legally obligated to provide. *Geller v. Geller.*

        <u>Reasons</u>: This exception is a fair and sensible limitation to total parental immunity. It penalizes parents only when they have negligently failed to supervise and care for their child, with certain exceptions, none of which are relevant in this case. The Lees were negligent in allowing their child to play alone with a chemistry set that had no instructions.

        <u>Counterargument</u>: Such a rule allows the state to intrude in matters better left to the parents—how to raise and care for their children. The immunity rule arose because of society's abhorrence of state intrusion into such private and sensitive matters.

        <u>Response</u>: The state does not intrude when parents are meeting obligations to their children that society has imposed on them.

    (2) <u>Position</u>: Alternatively, the court should replace total parental immunity with the "reasonable parent" rule. Parents are liable when "they do or fail to do what an ordinary and reasonably prudent parent would do in similar circumstances." *Peterson v. Peterson.*

<u>Reasons</u>: This rule is fair because it treats parents the same as other tortfeasors.

<u>Counterargument</u>: This theory allows for even more state intrusion than the *Geller* rule. It would apply to all phases of parenthood, including disciplining children and supervising their play. The *Peterson* court said that "a parent should be able to spank a child . . . without being sued for battery," yet that is a possibility under the reasonable parent rule the court adopted. A jury could decide, for example, that spanking a child is *per se* unreasonable, or that sending a child to her room is unreasonable. This rule is entirely too broad and is not in the best interests of the family.

<u>Response</u>: The reasonable parent rule imposes on parents the same obligation that it imposes on society generally—one who has a duty of care may not breach that duty without liability—except that it applies only to a breach of a parent's duty of care to the child. It is not an untoward state intrusion into private matters. In this case, the rule would operate as it should. The parents would not be immune from the consequences of negligently caring for their child.

(3) <u>Position</u>: Alternatively, the court should abolish parental immunity altogether.

<u>Reasons</u>: The concept is outmoded because the reasons for the rule no longer exist or never existed to begin with. First, the rationale that intra-family tort actions diminish family resources is no longer valid because most damage awards are paid by insurance companies. Second, there is no more danger of collusive lawsuits between parent and child than between other parties. Third, there is no more disruption of family harmony by tort actions than by property or contract disputes, yet these actions are allowed between parent and child.

[The counterarguments and responses to the counterarguments are outlined in the answer to 2(c).]

(d) Students should draft the argument based on the outline used to answer 2(c). You might have students exchange their arguments with students representing the Lees.

22
Point Headings

Changes From the Second Edition

There are no significant changes from the second edition.

Teaching Notes

A useful exercise is to have students turn the Questions Presented in an office memo they have written into point headings for a brief. To illustrate the differences in objective and persuasive writing, you might ask questions such as: Would you change the order of the issues? Are there any issues you would not include because the argument would be weak? How would you change the description of the issues and significant facts? To continue this exercise, assign half your class to write for each party in the case. You can then discuss how differences in emphasis, organization and word choice can be used to make a point heading more persuasive

Suggested Approach to Exercises

Exercise 22-A

Some students identify a threshold issue concerning whether Hinkle's injury was self-inflicted. Because self-infliction is not part of the quoted statutory language, and because the text emphasizes the importance of quoting the language at issue, other students will not identify this as a threshold issue. If students raise this as an issue, you can discuss it as the most significant one for the Commission. If the Commission can prove that the injury was self-inflicted, it wins the case and subsequent arguments about worker's compensation coverage are irrelevant. Hinkle, on the other hand, would have to argue that (1) the injury was not self-inflicted, and (2) even if it was, the term should not include accidental and unintended injury to oneself during horseplay. Both parties would place this point first regardless of its strength or significance, because logic demands that a threshold issue be addressed before issues that depend on its resolution. Thus, the outline of points for each side would be divided into two:

    I.   The injury was/was not self-inflicted.

    II.   The injury did/did not arise out of or in the course of Hinkle's employment.

One way to teach this problem is to assign Hinkle's side to half the class and the Commission's side to the other half. Then ask each student to turn in point headings for their client's argument. A teacher can then copy (or use an overhead projector) to show selected student-written point headings, ask students which point headings they prefer and why, and identify good and bad approaches.

Below are sample point headings for the second issue, two from each side, from a classroom discussion. Although more than four answers were used in this discussion, these four illustrate some basic points.

The point headings for both parties as to the second issue should follow the same basic outline. Hinkle's general statement that the Industrial Commission erred in denying his claim, and the Commission's general statement that it properly denied Hinkle's claim, should each be followed by specific assertions that correspond to the factors in the *Sperry* case. The specific assertions show why the general assertion is true. They should include the reason for the assertion and the key facts relevant to that assertion.

H-1

HINKLE IS ENTITLED TO COMPENSATION FOR HIS EYE INJURY.

A.   Shooting rubber bands was not a serious and lengthy departure from Hinkle's job because it was for a short period of time.

B.   Shooting rubber bands was not a complete deviation from the performance of the job because it was a short distraction.

C.   Shooting rubber bands has become part of Hinkle's employment because it has happened a number of times.

D.   The nature of Hinkle's employment can be expected to include some horseplay because of the ready availability of rubber bands.

H-2

THE INDUSTRIAL COMMISSION ERRED IN DENYING HINKLE'S WORKER'S COMPENSATION BENEFITS BECAUSE HIS INJURY AROSE "OUT OF OR IN THE COURSE OF" HIS EMPLOYMENT.

A.   Hinkle was injured in a minor and brief departure from his job.

B.   Hinkle was injured while performing his regular work.

C.   Hinkle was injured while engaged in recurring horseplay of which his supervisor was aware.

D.   Hinkle's employment can be expected to include some horseplay because of the ready availability of rubber bands.

THE TRIAL COURT WAS CORRECT IN
NOT ASSESSING AN AWARD FOR HINKLE.

A. Hinkle should not receive benefits under Section 45 of the State Worker's Compensation Act because his injuries did not occur in the normal course of his employment with Goff Medical Supply Co.

B. Hinkle does not meet the four factors necessary to establish a claim under the Worker's Compensation Act.

   1. The injury in this case resulted from an extended amount of time away from the work area.

   2. There was completeness in deviation because the horseplay was unrelated to his employment as a deliverer of medical supplies.

   3. The "fights" had occurred on more than one occasion and the employees had been warned against them in the past; thus, the horseplay had become a regular occurrence.

   4. Although the rubber bands may lend themselves to horseplay, an eighteen-inch piece of wood hardly constitutes something readily available for horseplay.

THE INDUSTRIAL COMMISSION PROPERLY DENIED
HINKLE'S WORKER'S COMPENSATION BENEFITS.

A. Hinkle was injured during a serious deviation from his job.

B. Hinkle was injured during a complete deviation from his job because, while he should have been loading a truck, he was engaged in a rubber band fight with another employee.

C. Hinkle was injured while engaged in horseplay that his supervisor had discouraged.

D. Horseplay cannot be expected to be part of Hinkle's employment because there is no evidence of lulls in activity.

This classroom discussion began with a question about which of the "H" point headings the students liked best. This elicited strong support for "H-2." The teacher then asked why. The answers here tended to correspond to the principles in the text.

The teacher then asked questions about specific headings. Which main heading on Hinkle's behalf is better? Why? The heading under "H-2" is better, the teacher explained, because it frames the question in terms of the Commission's alleged error. (This question, of course, anticipates Chapter 25 (Briefs to an Appellate Court).)

The teacher then asked questions about the subheadings. The questions focused on which subheadings under each were better. In "H-1," students tended to prefer A and D to the more vague B ("short distraction") and C ("has happened a number of times"). The more vague the point headings, of course, the less persuasive they are. In "H-2," students tended to like all the subheadings but could not explain, when specifically asked, how A differed from B.

The teacher then asked about the "I" point headings. Most liked "I-2" best. Their reasons were drawn from the text. There was discussion about the main heading, which differs from the main heading under "H-2" because it doesn't contain any reason. The main heading under "H-2" is better because it provides a general reason that connects the statutory text to the four factors.

There are several problems with "I-1." The main heading refers to the trial court when it should refer to the Industrial Commission. Students need to understand that government agencies often make the initial decision in these cases. In addition, use of the word "assessing" is inappropriate. Subheading B.3., moreover, appears to argue Hinkle's position. The main heading and the subheading marked A should be combined and distilled; they are repetitive as is. The sentence after B, moreover, is unnecessary. Some of the sentences under the headings marked 1 through 4 are wordy and awkward. These problems come out in class discussion, and students gain confidence by successfully identifying problems in someone else's work.

Basing an exercise on student papers, of course, requires the teacher to be responsive to the particular strengths and weaknesses of those papers. To do this properly, the teacher needs to study the papers beforehand.

The division of the second issue into four subheadings is logical in light of the four factors adopted in *Sperry*. Some of our students have thought it more logical, however, to combine factor one (extent and seriousness of the deviation) with factor two (completeness of the deviation). They see no difference between them except in degree. The difference is fairly subtle. The first factor describes horseplay commingled with the performance of duties. The second factor describes complete abandonment of duties so that the worker can concentrate all his energies on the horseplay. As the deviation becomes more extensive and more serious, the line between these two factors tends to blur. A lengthy and serious deviation could be a complete abandonment. (See the case cited in the Bibliography of the main text, under Exercise 22-A.)

As the example under principle 3 in the text illustrates, it is sometimes best to combine two closely related points. The student should not make this decision until he or she has analyzed the issues, outlined or drafted the argument, and considered the overall strategy of the brief. Principle 3 suggests several questions you should ask students to consider in this situation. For example: Are the arguments supporting each point so repetitive that they should be combined? Are the arguments for each stronger if they are combined? Is it good strategy to combine the two?

Exercise 22-B

The order for the main points of the respective arguments are given in the answers to Exercise 21-C. Below are outlines of the arguments for each side. The point headings should be more polished versions of these points.

Lees' argument:

(1)   This state's doctrine of parental immunity precludes PlayChem's defense that the parents were contributorily negligent.

(2)   The doctrine serves important public policies that would be undermined by adoption of the *Geller* rule or the reasonable parent rule.

        a.   Parent-child lawsuits disrupt family harmony.
        b.   Parent-child lawsuits deplete family resources.
        c.   Parental immunity prevents collusive lawsuits.
        d.   Parent-child lawsuits allow the state to intrude in matters best left to parents.

(3)   Even under the *Geller* rule, the parents are immune from suit because they were not furnishing basic necessities required by law.

PlayChem's argument:

(1)   A defendant in a tort action brought by a child should be allowed to assert the defense of contributory negligence by the parents when the parents' negligence in supervising and caring for the child caused or contributed to the injury.

        a.   This court should adopt a recognized exception to the parental immunity rule by imposing liability on parents unless they are providing to their child care that they are legally obligated to provide.

        b.   Alternatively, this court should adopt a reasonable-parent standard, which permits a child to sue a parent when the parent has failed to act as a reasonably prudent parent would act under similar circumstances.

(2)   The court should not apply the parental immunity rule in this case.

        a.   This state's courts have never applied the rule to defeat a claim of parental contributory negligence.

        b.   The parental immunity rule is an outmoded doctrine that has been rejected by many states because it serves no beneficial societal purpose.

(i)   The fear that intra-family suits would deplete family resources is no longer applicable because insurance companies pay most damage awards.

(ii)   Tort actions do not present a greater danger of disrupting family harmony than other kinds of lawsuits in which parental immunity does not apply.

(iii)   There is no more danger of collusive lawsuits between parent and child than between other parties to a lawsuit.

One problem in drafting point headings for PlayChem is that there are several alternative arguments. PlayChem has to argue that the court should adopt the *Geller* rule, or in the alternative adopt the *Peterson* rule, or in the alternative abolish parental immunity altogether. Use of too many "in the alternative" arguments is repetitious and may make the advocate appear indecisive. The outline of the PlayChem argument deals with this problem by casting the abolition argument not as another alternative but as a statement that the doctrine should not apply in this case.

23
Statement of Facts for a Brief

Changes From the Second Edition

We updated the example in the text and changed the name of the plaintiff. We also updated Exercise 23-A.

Teaching Notes

This chapter can also be reinforced with exercises similar to those suggested Chapter 22 (Point Headings): return to an objective memorandum that you assigned earlier in the course and draft several versions of the statement of facts. One approach is to convert an objective statement of facts to a persuasive statement of facts. Begin with a fairly good student-written example from the objective memorandum and have students work in small groups to draft a new fact statement from the perspective of one of the parties in the case. A second approach reverses the process. Begin by having students draft a persuasive statement of facts for one side or the other, then compare the two versions. Try to identify the persuasive techniques employed in each version, and then convert the two versions into a single objective statement of facts.

Suggested Approach to Exercises

Exercise 23-A

1. Because the problem requires a choice between two legal rules, the legally significant facts involve the applicability of each rule. Under the *Nokavich* case, parties are bound by the terms of their settlement. Thus, the terms and circumstances of the settlement agreement between Ellen Brummer and Ivan Pearce are legally significant. The exact language concerning "bodily injuries, known and unknown, and which have resulted or may in the future develop" is particularly important. The circumstances would include the fact of the accident, who was involved, and the eventual settlement.

   Under the *Brooks* case, a party can open a personal injury settlement for an injury of which neither party was aware when signing the settlement. Legally significant facts would include the specific injuries Nancy Brummer suffered that were known when the agreement was signed (facial lacerations, chip fracture in her nasal bones), the subsequent electroencephalogram showing her severe brain damage, and the special help or treatment she will require as a result of her brain damage (for her potential seizures, for her impaired reading and hand-eye coordination, and for her education).

2. Emotionally favorable facts for Brummer include her promising musical career and details about the injury.

3. Emotionally favorable facts for Pearce include details about what Ellen Brummer could have learned about Nancy's condition before signing the settlement, and her apparent understanding of what she signed.

4.   Important procedural facts include Ellen Brummer's attempt to persuade the trial court to reopen the settlement and the trial court's refusal to do so.

5.   In outline form, the Statement of Facts for Brummer should begin by describing five-year-old Nancy Brummer as a promising violinist. The specific details of the accident and the original settlement will follow. Then the subsequent test, coupled with her injuries and required care and treatment, should be described. The statement should end with an explanation of Ellen Brummer's unsuccessful effort to reopen the settlement.

6.   In outline form, the Statement of Facts for Pearce should begin with the accident and settlement. The details of the settlement would follow, including the fact that Ellen Brummer read the settlement before signing it. The statement would then describe the subsequent test, the results, and the care and treatment that will be required. It would include the doctor's statement that an electroencephalogram immediately after the accident would have disclosed the problem. It would conclude with the trial court's refusal to reopen the settlement and the court's statement that a settlement means what it says.

A teacher could contrast the two statements in several ways. One is to show students copies of opposing statements written by other students.

Exercise 23-B

1.   The legally significant facts include:

  ➤   The parents bought a chemistry set for their child.
  ➤   The child was five years old.
  ➤   The set had no instructions, though such sets usually came with instructions.
  ➤   The father requested instructions but did not receive them.
  ➤   The manufacturer attempted to send instructions when notified that they were missing but had the wrong address.
  ➤   The parents allowed the child to play with the set without supervision.
  ➤   Use of the set was not part of the child's formal schooling.
  ➤   The set was designed for use by children sixteen years old and older.
  ➤   While using the set, the child formed gunpowder and heated it, causing an explosion.
  ➤   The child was injured by the explosion.

2.   The emotional facts favorable to the Lees include:

  ➤   The child has a genius-level IQ.
  ➤   The child's teacher in a program for gifted children told the parents that the child had been taught some chemistry and could handle an advanced chemistry set.
  ➤   PlayChem manufacturer's chemistry sets primarily for educational purposes.
  ➤   The child was permanently blinded in her left eye by the accident.
  ➤   The accident severely and permanently disabled the child's right hand.
  ➤   Her injuries will preclude her from living a normal life in some respects.

3. The emotional facts favorable to PlayChem include:

> ➤ Many well-known scientists and Nobel Prize nominees got their start with a PlayChem chemistry set.
>
> ➤ As soon as PlayChem learned the instructions were missing, it immediately sent a copy to the address it was given.

4. The important procedural facts include:

> ➤ Susan Lee, a minor, brought suit against PlayChem alleging that she was injured by PlayChem's negligence in not including instructions in a chemistry set it manufactured and sold.
>
> ➤ PlayChem asserted as an affirmative defense that Susan's parents were contributorily negligent in giving the chemistry set to Susan and allowing her to use it without supervision, even though they knew the set had no instructions. It made a motion for partial summary judgment based on the parents' contributory negligence.
>
> ➤ The court denied PlayChem's motion, holding that the doctrine of parental immunity would bar the defense of contributory negligence against parents when the plaintiff is their child.

5. Students who are counsel for the Lees should begin by describing the Lee family, including their daughter, Susan, as well as Susan's intellectual abilities and her participation in the voluntary university program for gifted children. These facts should be stated in detail and should show that Susan was capable of using an advanced chemistry set despite her young age. Students should then state that the parents discussed the advanced chemistry set with her teacher, who told them he thought she could handle it. When the set Thomas Lee purchased had no instructions, he promptly called PlayChem and requested them. He did not receive them. Students should then describe accurately but in general terms the events leading to the explosion, including the Lee's lack of supervision. The statement should end with a detailed description of Susan's injuries and the effect these injuries will have on her future.

6. Students who are counsel for PlayChem should begin by describing the company, including specific details about its manufacture and marketing of chemistry sets. They should probably add that many scientists and Nobel Prize nominees got their start with PlayChem sets, which come in different levels of complexity. The statement should then briefly introduce the Lees, and describe in accurate but general terms Susan's intellectual abilities. The statement should describe in specific terms her age and her enrollment in a university program for gifted children. Students should then explain that the Lees purchased the most complicated of the PlayChem chemistry sets for Susan, a set designed for sixteen- to eighteen-year-old children. Students should explain the complexity of the set in detail. They should state that her father bought the set because she was good at science and had learned some chemistry at school. Although the set was missing instructions when the Lees purchased it, PlayChem immediately tried to send another copy. Even though the Lees did not receive the copy, they allowed Susan to use the set.

Students should conclude the statement with details concerning the parents' failure to supervise Susan's use of the set even though they knew there were no instructions. This part of the statement should also describe the accident in as little detail as possible, although it should be accurate.

Make sure students understand that the main objective is to tell a story that unfolds logically and is easy to follow. If logic requires placing an unfavorable fact in a place of emphasis, you might suggest that they weaken the impact by placing it in a subordinate clause. For example: "Although Susan was only five years old, she had a genius-level IQ and the intelligence of a much older child." You might also show examples of how to describe facts blandly or vividly. For example, the Lees would describe the set as an advanced chemistry set, while PlayChem would describe it as a highly complicated and dangerous set which contained seventy-eight different chemicals, a Bunsen burner and laboratory equipment, and which required detailed instructions.

24
Briefs to a Trial Court

Changes From the Second Edition

There are no significant changes from the second edition.

Teaching Notes

There are no additional teaching notes for this chapter.

Suggested Approach to Exercises

Exercise 24-A

Because the problem and cases are discussed so extensively in the text, we will only highlight some basic points here.

Aaron must argue that *Raseen* is applicable to this factual situation. The action for contribution here is part of the plaintiff's suit, not a separate action. Both *Sarasota* and *Rollins* should be distinguished on this basis. Additionally, Aaron has clearly indicated that settlement is not likely. These facts show that the two purposes behind the settlement-bar rule, avoiding additional litigation and promoting settlements, are not applicable here. Specific facts from the cases need to be compared in order to support these conclusions.

As part of the argument, Aaron should also challenge the overall fairness of the initial settlement. The $1.5 million Chisolm settled for is but a small percentage of the $10 million Miller seeks, even though the accident might have been prevented had Chisolm maintained the plane properly. Financial responsibility for damages, Aaron might argue, should be more evenly distributed. *Raseen* can be analogized and *Sarasota* distinguished on this point. *Rollins* is also distinguishable in that both tortfeasors had agreed to their settlement amounts. Again, it is important to contrast the specific facts of the cases. Even though Aaron has been offered the same settlement that Chisolm agreed to, Aaron should not be forced to choose between a settlement it does not believe is fair and potential liability for an amount that far exceeds its responsibility in this case. Aaron should highlight Chisolm's negligence in supporting this point.

The argument should be brief. Students should not need more than three or four double-spaced pages to make this argument.

Exercise 24-B

These comments should be read in conjunction with the suggested answers to Exercise 7-B.

Farmer's brief should focus on (1) the applicability of the legal rules because Farmer has a credible argument whether the court applies the "substantial possibility of recovery" standard or the "more likely than not" standard, and (2) the court's policy that a physician should not be held liable for a result that was a mere possibility. Quale's brief should focus more on (1) the applicability of the "more likely than not" standard in light of the expert's opinion regarding

157

Andrew's chance of survival, (2) the undoubtedly sympathetic facts of the case, and (3) the injustice of not holding a physician liable for the death of a child when a correct diagnosis and surgery could have saved him.

Both parties have strong policy and equity arguments; neither side has the advantage in this regard. Farmer has a slightly stronger legal position.

Exercise 24-C

Much of the analysis in this problem is shown in the answers to Exercises 8-D and 14-C(2) in this manual. The answers here are in outline form.

1. Because the League has the burden of showing that it is entitled to intervene, its brief must show that it complies with all three elements. The Chapter 21 principles for drafting an argument are a good place to start. Students need to think about the order of arguments on each sub-issue. Which is the strongest? We think possible or actual inadequacy of representation by existing parties is probably the strongest, especially after the city attorney's recent statement. Timeliness is probably next, and fits well here. The last argument should be based on the possibility that the League will be bound; the League is vulnerable to an argument that its interest is primarily ideological, but that concern seems less compelling in light of the first and second arguments. Teachers may want to discuss other aspects of advocacy here as well.

    The principles in Chapter 24 will also influence the drafting of the argument. The League's brief needs to show the trial court that the rule and the case law clearly apply to the facts of this case. Thus, it will base it argument mostly on the language of the rule and the facts of the *Halsey* case.

    The League's brief would thus emphasize the following facts in arguing that the three requirements of the statute are met:

    ▶   The city attorney's statement indicates not only that the city is not representing the League's interest but also that it is now on the side of rezoning. This goes beyond the minimum requirement, established in *Halsey*, that a party must only show that existing representation "may be" inadequate.

    ▶   The League filed its application promptly upon learning that its interest was no longer being represented by the city.

    ▶   If the application to intervene is denied, the League will be "bound" by the decision to rezone as that term has been defined in *Halsey*. Its ability to further pursue the possibility of locating low income housing in the targeted area will be "substantially affected" by the salvage yard and by the other commercial ventures that will seek rezoning if Swift is successful. This, in turn, will substantially affect the ability of the League's members to occupy the low-income housing envisioned for the targeted area.

The argument must also show the League in a sympathetic light. That can be done, in the context of the sub-issue concerning whether the League may be bound, by describing the League's long involvement with this eighteen-square-block area and the potential domino effect that approval of Swift's application would have. Students should understand that they
bring in sympathetic facts while they make legal arguments, not merely to show the League as sympathetic.

The argument should also be brief. Students should be able to write the argument in about two double-spaced pages, if not less. The brevity of the argument, of course, makes it attractive as a teaching tool.

Students will not know who the judge is, and so the fourth principle is irrelevant. Teachers might invent a judge with a particular disposition and ask students how this judge's disposition would influence the drafting of the brief.

2. Swift's counsel has an interesting tactical decision to make at the beginning. Should he or she fight the League on all three sub-issues, or just one or two? After all, defeating just one element means Swift wins. Some students will find that possibility attractive, but others will see that they have more opportunities to win if they contest the League on all three.

The strongest argument for Swift is probably based on the possibility that the applicant may be bound, and relies on the assertion that the League's interest is primarily ideological. Its weakest argument probably concerns timeliness. The arguments should be ordered accordingly.

Swift's brief will also focus on the three requirements of the statute, but will emphasize the following facts to show how they are not met here:

► The League does not have an interest here that is sufficient to support intervention. This suit is between a private landowner and the city. The League neither owns nor occupies property in this area. Thus, it will not be "substantially affected" by a decision in this case.

► Assuming that League members have some interest as citizens, the interests of its members are adequately represented by the city, which represents the interests of all citizens.

► Swift filed this action six months ago; the League has waited too long to try to intervene at this point. The application is not timely.

Swift can argue the fairness of its position by emphasizing that this suit will be unnecessarily complicated by the introduction of another adverse party and that the facts indicated above show the League does not really need or deserve the right to intervene. It should also emphasize facts that reduce sympathy for the League. When it argues that the League will not be bound, for example, it should emphasize that the League owns none of the relevant property and that none of its members appears to own any of the relevant property. It should also suggest the positive economic and job-creating value of an auto salvage yard. Swift's argument should not take more than about two double-spaced pages.

3. This question is meant to identify possible differences between the city's position and Swift's position. Because Swift sued the city over the zoning decision, they are on opposite sides of an existing lawsuit. Each will try to evaluate whether the League's intervention helps them or hurts them. If the city agrees with Swift, of course, these differences collapse.

    This raises the possibility that the League's brief will be opposed by two briefs, not one. Students will have different views about whether that matters. The city's brief will focus on many of the same facts that Swift's brief included and will emphasize the following facts:

    ➤   The city has not indicated that it will not adequately represent the League's interest. The city has stated all along that it will represent all of the people, which includes the interests of the members of the League.

    The city has not indicated any drastic change in its position that would justify the League's sudden concern because, from the outset, the city indicated only that the proposal was "worth looking into," not that it unqualifiedly supported the idea. Thus, the application is not timely because there is no justification for the League's six-month delay. The city can argue the fairness of its position by emphasizing its ability and intent to represent the interests of all of its citizens. Further, adding another adverse party to this suit will bring unnecessary delays and complications to what is essentially a dispute between the city and a private landowner.

4. Have the students weigh the various arguments raised and explain why they believe one is stronger than the others. Remember that policy plays a lesser role in a trial court than in an appellate court, but it nonetheless may be considered. That this question pits a landowner/business owner against a poorer segment of society may carry some weight in a trial court.

    The League's position is probably stronger. The League has decent supportable arguments under each element. The policies underlying the intervention rule seem to tip doubtful cases toward the person seeking to intervene. Given the League's long history with this particular tract, that result also seems fair.

25
Briefs to an Appellate Court

Changes From the Second Edition

There are no major changes from the second edition.

Teaching Notes

There are no additional teaching notes for this chapter.

Suggested Approach to Exercises

Exercise 25-A

Because the problem is discussed so extensively in the text, we will only highlight some basic points here.

Aaron's brief, like Chisolm's, should be drafted in view of the standard of review. Aaron should subtly emphasize that even though the standard is *de novo,* the trial court's opinion should be accorded a great deal of weight because of the role of the trial court in the fact-finding process.

Aaron would argue the analogies and distinctions of the *Raseen*, *Sarasota*, and *Rollins* cases as it did in the trial court, but with more emphasis placed on the policies behind the rule. Aaron's position should be established as consistent with *Raseen* and the more recent trend in the law.

Aaron should capitalize on the reasoning of the trial court's opinion by showing that the policies supporting the settlement bar rule would not be furthered here and that its application is unfair in view of the specific facts of this case. Aaron would also include a more detailed argument on the potential unfairness of the settlement-bar rule, and the impossible choice that Aaron is faced with because Chisolm has settled. That is, Aaron must either accept the offered settlement or risk potential liability for far more than its share of Miller's damages. The Burns article offers support for this argument, and students should use it. Students should also characterize Aaron's position as representative of the position any joint tortfeasor may face, because appellate courts are concerned with the precedent this case will set as well as with the outcome in this particular case.

Exercise 25-B

Note on organization of the issues in Greenleaf's brief: According to the rule that one places the strongest argument first, Greenleaf would begin with the argument that Elliot unreasonably interfered with his right to the free flow of light because it is much stronger than the argument that he has such a right, However, because the right to the free flow of light is a threshold issue, we decided that logic trumped the relative persuasive value of the arguments in this case.

1 /2. The trial court found in Greenleaf's favor except as to the legal right to the free flow of light. Therefore, Greenleaf would only appeal the judge's ruling that he has no such legal right Elliot would then cross-appeal from the ruling that Greenleaf suffered damages sufficient for a nuisance action.

3 /4. Each argument would be drafted along the lines suggested in the answers to Exercise 7-C, as follows:

Outline of argument for Greenleaf:

(1) This state should recognize a legal right to the free flow of light.

    a. The rule in *Shover* is broad enough to include the right to the free flow of light. There is no meaningful difference between the right to lateral support and the right to the flow of sunlight.

    b. The rule in *Cassells* that there is no right to the free flow of light is not binding and should be rejected.

        (i) The rule was formulated before society's interest in encouraging the development of alternative energy sources. This interest greatly outweighs policy reasons underlying the *Cassells* rule.

        (ii) *Cassells* is distinguishable. The damage to Greenleaf is relatively much greater than the damage suffered in *Cassells*. There, the hotel owner anticipated potential economic loss and inconvenience to its guests. Here, Greenleaf's business might be destroyed because potential customers can see that solar energy will not work if neighbors can block the sunlight. Even if Greenleaf's business survives, the potential damage is similar to that in *Shover*, where the loss of lateral support "greatly devalued" the property.

(2) Elliot unreasonably interfered with Greenleaf's right to the free flow of light by erecting billboards that block the sun from Greenleaf's solar panels.

    a. The interference is unreasonable because it is destroying Greenleaf's business. This case is analogous to *Blum* and *Horton*. In *Blum*, noise and vibrations from a landfill owner's trucks caused the conception rate of the sows on a neighboring hog farm to decrease from 80% to 30%. The court held that the landfill owner's use of his land was unreasonable and a nuisance because it essentially destroyed the hog farm. In *Horton* the court assessed damages against a landowner who dusted his crops with a spray that was toxic to a neighboring farmer's bees because the spraying was an unreasonable interference with the neighbor's peaceful enjoyment of his property. Like the trash-hauling trucks in *Blum* and the toxic spray in *Horton*, Elliot's billboards are essentially destroying Greenleaf's property by making his promotional appeal less attractive and by increasing his cost of doing business substantially.

b.   In balancing the interests of the parties, the trial court properly concluded that Greenleaf's interest in continuing his architectural business and promoting solar energy outweighs Elliot's interest in erecting advertising billboards. The court's conclusion was correct for two reasons. First, as the *Blum* court makes clear, the balance will always be struck in favor of the one whose business is being destroyed. Second, Greenleaf's business has more value to the community than Elliot's business. Greenleaf employs twelve people and is also promoting a product that reduces environmental pollution.

Outline of argument for Elliot:

(1)   There is no legal right to the free flow of light.

a.   The rule in *Cassells* is the common law rule. No American court has ever recognized a right to the flow of light. *Shover* is inapplicable because it concerned the right to lateral support.

b.   The reasons for the rule are just as valid today. Requiring that every property owner allow the free flow of sunlight onto neighboring property would make building construction in high-density areas economically unfeasible. It would also infringe on individual property rights.

c.   The *Cassells* case is analogous. Both Greenleaf and the hotel owner in *Cassells* suffered some economic damage and some inconvenience in carrying on their respective businesses. As the *Cassells* court recognized, such damage does not warrant recognizing a new legal right and overturning a universally recognized common law rule.

(2)   The billboards do not constitute a nuisance because they are a mere inconvenience to Greenleaf, not an unreasonable interference with his architectural business.

a.   The interests of each landowner must be balanced. The consequences to Elliot if he is required either to remove his billboards or to pay damages to Greenleaf would be serious. It would amount to a partial destruction of his business, a result similar to the result the *Blum* court called unreasonable. In *Horton* the activity was unreasonable because the crop duster could have easily prevented the damage by spraying on a calm day. Elliot, however, cannot prevent the damage to Greenleaf without substantial cost.

b.   The interference with Greenleaf's solar panels is not unreasonable. It is not a virtual destruction of his business, as was the case in *Blum*, nor a destruction of part of the property, as was the case in *Horton*. Greenleaf's advertising promotion may have suffered and his utility bills may be higher, but these are reasonable consequences of accommodating the interests of both parties.

5.   Answers will vary. One approach is to ask students to play the role of judge. Give them a student argument for each side and ask them to decide the case. Ask them what they liked and did not like about the briefs they read.

We think it likely that the practical (and unknown) consequences of a right to free flow of light would persuade an appellate court to affirm Judge Shea's decision. We also believe Judge Shea would be affirmed on the unreasonable interference issue.

APPENDICES

The following appendices include two kinds of materials: (1) sample discussions, annotated to illustrate the principles in various chapters of the text, and (2) teaching aids.

Annotated Discussions

Appendices A through C contain five annotated discussions. Students often have trouble applying the lessons learned in class to their own writing. Understanding a thing and successfully doing the thing can be separated by hours of hard work, and this can be very frustrating for the new legal writer. One technique that many teachers use to help students internalize a lesson is the in-class "deconstruction" of a sample. We have included five such samples in Appendices A through C.

Appendix A has three sample discussions based on the contract problem that begins in Exercise 6-A of the text and continues in Exercises 11-A and 12-A. Appendix B contains one discussion based on the nuisance problem in Exercise 7-C of the text. Appendix C reproduces the first major section of the office memo in *Tyler v. Eastern Pacific University*, which appears as Appendix A in the text.

All five of these samples are annotated to show students where the author sets out the governing legal rule, describes the precedent cases, analyzes the issue, responds to opposing arguments, or employs organizational principles. You can review these annotated samples in class, but a better approach is to give your students a "clean" copy of the sample – *i.e.*, an unannotated version of the sample – and ask them to "deconstruct" it in class, focusing on the particular lesson you are working on. For example, you might first ask students to find and label the classic IRAC or CRAC components of the discussion in conjunction with Chapter 10 (Organization). Later you might ask them to identify thesis statements and topic sentences in conjunction with Chapter 13 (Signposting). As you work through the various samples, students will begin to recognize how the various lessons that you teach operate when put to use in a piece of writing.

Teaching Aids

Appendices D through F are designed to give you some ideas for teaching. Appendix D is an example of a grading/criteria sheet. Although this example is designed for Exercise 14-A, a similar grading sheet can be designed for many of the exercises in the text, or for other writing projects that you assign to your students. Appendix E focuses on Questions Presented and describes a three-step method for teaching your students how to construct good questions. Finally, Appendix F describes a pre-writing technique that helps students learn how to read, process, and organize the law and facts relevant to any new problem they are asked to solve.

Appendix A

SAMPLE ANNOTATED DISCUSSIONS
Exercises 6-A, 11-A, and 12-A

The examples below are based on the facts and law used in Exercises 6-A, 11-A, and 12-A. Examples 1 and 2 illustrate the analysis of the offer issue; Example 3 illustrates the analysis of the acceptance issue.

Example 1: Effective Offer

Assume that an introductory or thesis paragraph precedes this discussion and analyses of the acceptance and consideration elements follow it.

Thesis statement	McKay made an effective offer to sell his yacht to Green because Green reasonably believed McKay intended to make a binding offer, even though McKay did not actually have that intent.
Rule	An offer is effective in this state if the offeror intended to make a binding offer, but intent is defined not by what the offeror actually intended but by an objective standard: "[W]hether a reasonable person in the offeree's shoes would believe that the offeror intended to make a binding contract." <u>Derek v. Beir</u> (1985).
Facts, holding, and reasoning of <u>Derek</u>	In <u>Derek</u>, the offeror told the offeree, his neighbor, that for five dollars he would build a wall between their lots so that he would never have to look at the offeree's "ridiculous" face again. The offeree agreed and paid him five dollars, but the offeror never built the wall. The offeree in that case knew about the offeror's reputation for playing practical jokes on his neighbors. Under those circumstances, the court held that there was no binding offer

166

because the offeree either knew or should have known that the offeror was not serious. *Id.*

Facts, inferences, and reasoning distinguishing Derek and supporting conclusion

Unlike the offeree in <u>Derek</u>, who knew the offeror's reputation for playing practical jokes, Green did not know of McKay's reputation as a practical joker and so had no reason to doubt that the offer was genuine. His response at the end of the conversation that he needed time to think about the offer and raise the money shows that he took the offer seriously. This attitude was reasonable because McKay gave him no reason to doubt the sincerity of the offer.

Facts, inferences, and reasoning comparing Derek and explaining counter position

In both <u>Derek</u> and this case, the offeror named an absurd price. In <u>Derek</u>, the offeror promised to build a ten-foot-high wall between his lot and the offeree's lot for five dollars. McKay offered to sell his boat for one-tenth of its value. A reasonable person might have suspected that McKay's offer was not serious. Green, who knew the value of the boat, did express incredulity in response to the offer when he said, "You can't be serious." Yet McKay

Reason for rejecting counter position

continued the conversation after that and never intimated that the offer was a joke. Green's belief that McKay intended to make a

Conclusion

binding offer was therefore reasonable under the circumstances.

Example 2: Ineffective Offer

Assume that an introductory or thesis paragraph precedes this discussion and analyses of the acceptance and consideration elements follow it.

Thesis statement

McKay's offer to sell his yacht to Green was not effective because a reasonable person would not have believed he intended to make a binding contract. An offer is effective in this state if the

Rule

offeror intended to make a binding contract, but intent is defined not by what the offeror actually intended but by an objective standard: "[W]hether a reasonable person in the offeree's shoes would believe that the offeror intended to make a binding contract." Derek v. Beir (1985).

Facts, holding, and reasoning of Derek

In Derek, the offeror told the offeree, his neighbor, that for five dollars he would build a wall between their lots so that he would never have to look at the offeree's "ridiculous" face again. The offeree agreed and paid him five dollars but the offeror never built the wall. The offeree in that case knew about the offeror's reputation for playing practical jokes on his neighbors. Under those circumstances, the court held that there was no binding offer because the offeree either knew or should have known that the offeror was not serious. *Id.*

Facts, inferences, and reasoning comparing Derek and supporting conclusion

In Derek, the offeree attempted to enforce a contract based on a practical joke. The court rejected that attempt, holding that the offeree knew or should have known that the offeror's promise to build a ten-foot-high wall between their adjoining lots for five dollars was made in jest. *Id.* This case is similar. As a joke, McKay offered to sell his $50,000 yacht to Green for $5,000. In both cases, the value of the subject of the offer was greatly disproportionate to the price. Furthermore, Green knew the actual value of the boat. In fact, he responded to the offer by exclaiming, "You can't be serious." This response probably indicates Green's belief that McKay did not intend to make a binding contract. Any reasonable person in Green's shoes should have known the offer was not serious.

Facts, inferences, and reasoning distinguishing Derek *and explaining the counter position*

Nevertheless, Green may have believed that McKay intended to make a binding offer. Unlike the offeree in <u>Derek</u>, he did not know of the offeror's reputation as a practical joker. Also, during the conversation he requested time to consider the offer and raise the money. He probably would not have made this request unless he thought the offer was serious. If he had that belief,

Reason for rejecting counter position and conclusion

however, it was not reasonable because of the great disparity between the boat's value and the offered price.

Example 3: Valid Acceptance

Assume that analysis of the offer element precedes this discussion and analysis of the consideration element follows it.

Transition/thesis statement

Rule

The second requirement of an enforceable contract was met because Green accepted McKay's offer. A valid acceptance must be sufficiently communicated, and it must mirror the offer in every respect. Anselm v. Kinnet Textiles, Inc. (1986).

Thesis sentence regarding the first requirement

Facts, holding, and reasoning of Anselm relevant to sufficient communication

Green's acceptance over the telephone of McKay's offer was sufficient In Anselm, the offeree communicated his acceptance of Anselm's offer to sell cotton by giving a note to Anselm's secretary, who placed it on Anselm's cluttered desk. Anselm did not see the note for several weeks and committed the cotton to another buyer. The court rejected Anselm's argument that there was no acceptance because he did not read the note. It found that placement of the note on his desk was sufficient communication because "it would be unreasonable to require the offeree to ensure that the acceptance is read." Id.

Facts, inferences, and reasoning supporting conclusion

Similarly, it would be unreasonable in this case to require the offeree to ensure that his acceptance was heard. Green delivered his acceptance in the same way the offer was made--by telephone. He called McKay's office and left a message for McKay that he had called. McKay returned Green's call from the clubhouse at a golf course. He had been drinking and passed out before he heard Green's acceptance. Because McKay initiated the call, Green could not have known that McKay lost consciousness soon after that. He delivered the message, just as the offeree in Anselm did,

Analogy to Anselm

and he had no duty to make sure McKay received it.

Distinction of Anselm – facts, inferences, and reasoning supporting counter position

This case differs from <u>Anselm</u>, however, because the acceptance in <u>Anselm</u> was written rather than oral. Although it is unreasonable to expect one who sends a written message to ensure that the recipient reads it, it is not as unreasonable to expect one talking on the telephone to make sure that the other party hears the message. When McKay did not reply, Green could have suspected that something was wrong, but unless McKay's manner of speech indicated he was drunk, Green should not be expected to know that he had passed out and was thus incapable of hearing the message.

Reason for rejecting counter position

Because the <u>Anselm</u> court focused on whether the offeree sufficiently communicated his acceptance, not on whether the offeror received it, Green's oral acceptance to McKay is likely to be considered sufficient communication.

Thesis statement as to second requirement of acceptance

Green's acceptance also met the requirement in this state that "the acceptance must mirror the offer in every respect." <u>Id.</u> If the acceptance varies from the offer, it is a counteroffer and not an acceptance. <u>Id.</u> In <u>Anselm</u>, the offeror, Anselm, offered to sell 200 bales of cotton to Kinnet Textiles, Inc., with one hundred bales to be delivered on March 1 and another hundred on April 1. Kinnet sent a messenger to Anselm's office with a written note that stated: "We agree to your offer in all respects if we can instead take delivery on March 5 and April 5." The court held that the attempted acceptance was invalid because the acceptance differed from the offer. <u>Id.</u>

Facts, holding, and reasoning of Anselm relevant to mirror image rule

Facts, inferences, and reasoning supporting conclusion and distinguishing Anselm

Green's acceptance did not vary from the original offer. He called McKay on the telephone and said, "I accept the offer." The offeree in <u>Anselm</u>, on the other hand, said that he agreed to the offer <u>if</u> the dates were changed. This condition turned the attempted acceptance into a counteroffer. After Green accepted the offer, he said, "But I'd like to see your golf clubs thrown into the deal, too." Because Green used the verb "like," this statement was a suggestion or request rather that a condition or demand for additional goods.

Facts, inferences, and reasoning supporting counter position

Nevertheless, Green did use the conjunction "but," which might be considered a conditional term. If so the statement would be a demand for additional goods. "Acceptance conditioned on the seller's delivering additional goods not specified in his offer is a counteroffer and a rejection." Edna C. Simpson, <u>Contracts</u> 30-31 (3d ed. 2006). It is not likely, though, that Green would put a

Reasons for rejecting counter position

condition on acceptance of an offer that was quite advantageous to him. It is more likely that he was either joking or trying to see how far McKay's generosity would extend. Thus, his acceptance mirrored the offer because it did not demand inclusion of additional

Conclusion as to second requirement

goods.

Green's acceptance of McKay's offer to sell the yacht was valid. Green sufficiently communicated an unconditional

Conclusion as to acceptance

acceptance when he said, "I accept the offer."

172

Appendix B

SAMPLE ANNOTATED DISCUSSION
Exercise 7-C

Thesis statement

Bradley Greenleaf has no cause of action in nuisance against Peter Elliot, a neighboring property owner who erected two billboards that block the flow of sunlight to Greenleaf's solar panels. The rule in

Rule regarding legal right

this state is that landowners "must so enjoy their property as not to injure . . . a legal right in the property of another." Shover v. Scott

Synthesized rule defining action for nuisance

(1889). An action for nuisance will lie if: (1) the owner interferes with a legal right of another property owner, Shover; (2) the other owner suffers injury, Horton v. Eicher (1959); and (3) the interference is unreasonable, id.; Blum v. Disposal Systems, Inc. (1997). Even though the billboards are an unreasonable interference with Greenleaf's use and enjoyment of his property and have damaged his business financially, Elliot did not interfere with a recognized legal right.

Thesis statement regarding the first (threshold) issue

Greenleaf has no legal right to the free flow of light. In Shover, the court recognized a legal right to lateral support. Thus, the plaintiff

Shover case description

had a cause of action for damages he sustained when an owner of adjoining property excavated his land and caused the plaintiff's land to cave in. Id. No American court, however, has recognized a legal right to the free flow of light. Cassells v. Avery (1959). Citing this lack of

Cassells case description

precedent, the court in Cassells refused to recognize a legal right to the free flow of light in a case where a hotel owner's proposed ten-story addition would cast a shadow on the adjoining hotel owner's sunbathing areas. Id.

Analogy to Cassells and facts, inferences, and reasoning supporting writer's conclusion

While the Cassells case is from another jurisdiction, it deals with the exact question at issue here. Greenleaf will suffer economic hardship, as did the hotel owner in Cassells, unless the court recognizes a right to the free flow of light. The court is unlikely to do so. The economic damage in the two cases is similar. Greenleaf paid $300,000 to renovate the building housing his architectural firm and to fit it with solar panels. His specialty is solar design for residences. Not only will Greenleaf's costs of doing business increase, but the appeal of his solar energy promotion will also be less attractive because potential customers will realize that solar panels can be blocked from the sunlight by neighbors who erect billboards or buildings, or who plant tall trees. The hotel owner in Cassells would suffer economic damage because the neighboring hotel's addition would shadow its beaches and sunbathing areas, making them less attractive to hotel guests. The Cassells court pointed out that the doctrine of nuisance requires that a landowner injure the legal rights of another. Id. Because the court did not recognize a legal right to the flow of light, it refused to enjoin the neighbor's addition.

Facts, inferences, and reasoning supporting opposite conclusion

To prevail, Greenleaf must convince the court to recognize a new legal right--the right to the free flow of sunlight. The court in Shover recognized the right to lateral support. The distinction between

174

the right to lateral support and the right to the flow of light is arguably artificial. In each case, a practice that infringes on the right could cause severe economic harm. Furthermore, it is in the interest of today's society to encourage the development of alternative energy sources, an interest which was not considered by the court in <u>Cassells</u>.

Reasons for rejecting counterargument

Nevertheless, the reason for the rule in <u>Cassells</u> is just as valid today as it was in 1959. Requiring that every landowner allow the free flow of sunlight onto neighboring property would make building construction, especially in high density areas, economically unfeasible. It might even prohibit the planting of certain trees. Greenleaf has no strong argument for a change in the law, and in the absence of a strong or compelling

Conclusion and reasons for conclusion

argument, the court is unlikely to expand the rule in <u>Shover</u> to include a legal right to the free flow of sunlight.

Transition to second issue and thesis statement

Rule

If the court recognizes a legal right to the free flow of sunlight, it will consider the billboards that block the light from Greenleaf's solar panels a nuisance. "A property owner is entitled to the peaceful enjoyment of his property free from unreasonable interference by others." <u>Horton</u>.

Facts, reasoning, and holding of <u>Horton</u>

The nuisance in <u>Horton</u> was a toxic spray. A farmer who grew honeydew melons used a crop duster to spray his melons with calcium arsenate, a pesticide. Horton, also a farmer, kept sixty-five bee hives on a nearby parcel of land. The spray drifted onto Horton's land and killed the bees. The court found that the bees contributed to Horton's

175

livelihood because he used them to cross pollinate his plants. Id. It

affirmed the award of damages for a nuisance, holding that the drifting

of the spray was an unreasonable interference with the farmer's use of

his property. Id. The damage to Greenleaf's operation is similar. In

both cases one person's use of his property adversely affected the

livelihood of another person. Moreover, Elliot's erection of the

billboards is arguably a more serious interference with Greenleaf's

economic activity than the killing of a farmer's bees because the

damage is permanent, rather than temporary, as was the case in Horton.

An action that precludes Greenleaf from promoting his business is,

under the Horton rule, unreasonable.

In Blum, the court focused on the balance between the

respective interests of adjacent landowners. The court found that a

landfill operator's use of his land unreasonably interfered with his

neighbor's hog farm operation when noise and vibrations generated by

trash hauling trucks caused the conception rate of the neighbor's sows

to decrease from eighty to thirty percent. The court held that the landfill

operation was not "a mere annoyance or inconvenience" but a nuisance.

Id. "[A] use of property that essentially confiscates or destroys the

neighboring property is unreasonable and constitutes a nuisance." Id.

Balancing the interests of the respective owners in this case presents a

close question. The billboard owner has an interest in using his

property to its best advantage. Requiring him to remove the billboards

Analogy to Horton; facts, inferences, reasoning that conclusion

Explanation of Blum court's interpretation and application of unreasonable interference element

Application of Blum balancing test

might cause him to lose substantial business. Although the billboards

Objective comparison of facts to those in Blum

reduce the effectiveness of Greenleaf's solar energy promotional appeal and increase his costs substantially, they do not amount to as drastic a destruction of his business interests as was the case in Blum, where the farmer's sows suffered a decrease in conception rate of more than fifty percent. The competing economic interests of the parties in this case

Conclusion and reasons

are more evenly balanced than in Blum, but they weigh more heavily in Greenleaf's favor. His economic losses, over the years, are likely to be more than the billboard owner's losses.

Conclusion as to both issues and summary of reasons

Greenleaf will not succeed in an action against the billboard owner because Greenleaf has no legal right to the free flow of sunlight. Therefore, he has suffered no injury recognized at law. If the court does recognize such a legal right, Greenleaf is likely to win in a nuisance suit against his neighbor. The erection of the billboards is an unreasonable interference with Greenleaf's right to light. The blockage of the sunlight from his solar panels has already increased his energy cost substantially and will harm his business in the future. In balancing the interests of the landowners, the court is likely to find that the billboard owner's economic loss if he is forced to remove the billboards is outweighed by the harm he has inflicted on Greenleaf.

Appendix C

ANNOTATED DISCUSSION SHOWING ORGANIZATIONAL TECHNIQUES
See Text Appendix A, Section I.A.

Annotations on the left show basic organizational principles discussed in Chapter 10 (Organization). Annotations on the right show how the writer uses transitions and other signposts discussed in Chapter 13 (Signposting).

I. Negligent Misrepresentation

Conclusion on negligent misrep. claim

Timothy Tyler can probably recover damages caused by Richard Cramer's negligent misrepresentation that the Global Policy Studies (GPS) program had a preferential admission policy for Eastern Pacific University graduates. Damages for misrepresentation are recoverable under Cal. Civ. Code § 1709 (West 1998): "One who

Rule on negligent misrep.

willfully deceives another with intent to induce him to alter his position to his injury or risk, is liable for any damage which he thereby suffers." Deceit is defined to include: "The assertion, as a fact, of that which is not true, by one who has no reasonable ground for believing it to be true." Id. § 1710(2). One type of deceit or fraud is negligent misrepresentation. B.L.M. v. Sabo & Deitsch, 64 Cal. Rptr. 2d 335, 342 (Ct. App. 1997). As construed by the courts, a plaintiff making a negligent misrepresentation claim must prove each of the following elements: "(1) A misrepresentation of a past or existing material fact, (2) without reasonable grounds for believing it to be true, (3) with intent to induce another's reliance on the fact misrepresented, (4) ignorance of the truth and justifiable reliance thereon by the party to whom the misrepresentation was directed, and (5) damages." Id. (quoting Fox v. Pollack, 226 Cal. Rptr. 532, 537 (Ct. App. 1986)).

Enumerated points, 1-5

Writer disposes of the 2 "givens"

In this case, two elements are easily established. First, Cramer freely admitted that he made the statement to induce Tyler to enroll at Eastern Pacific, thereby establishing an intent to induce reliance.

Enumerated points, 1ˢᵗ & 2nd

178

, Tyler suffered damages in giving up his full scholarship at Crater Lake College to attend Eastern Pacific. He received only a nominal scholarship amount and had to pay most of Eastern Pacific's tuition himself. He also suffered damages because he was not given priority in his application to the GPS program. Therefore, three questions remain: **A)** whether Cramer's statement was a misrepresentation of an existing fact or only his opinion, **B)** whether Cramer lacked reasonable grounds for believing his statement to be true, and **C)** whether Tyler was justified in believing the statement to be true and relying on it.

Issues to be discussed

Enumerated points, A-C

A. Cramer's statement will probably be considered a statement of fact rather than an opinion because he held himself out as a trained professional on this subject. A misrepresentation must be one of existing fact; a statement as to value or other casual expression of belief is not actionable. See <u>Gentry v. eBay, Inc.</u>, 121 Cal. Rptr. 2d 703, 718–19 (Ct. App. 2002). **However**, a statement made by one who possesses or holds himself out as possessing superior knowledge or information regarding the subject of the statement may be treated as one of fact where the statement, although in the form of an opinion, is "a deliberate affirmation of the matters stated." <u>Bily v. Arthur Young & Co.</u>, 834 P.2d 745, 768 (Cal. 1992) (quoting <u>Gagne v. Bertran</u>, 275 P.2d 15, 21 (Cal. 1954)).

Conclusion on issue A

Rule on issue A

Relationship between ideas = difference

The courts have applied this rule to conclude that an opinion by a trained professional may be a statement of fact in an action for negligent misrepresentation, while a casual opinion offered by one speaking outside of his expertise is not. **For example**, in <u>Shafer v. Berger, Kahn, Shafton, Moss, Figler, Simon & Gladstone</u>, 131 Cal. Rptr. 2d 777, 793 (Ct. App. 2003), the court held that a statement by legal counsel for an insurance company regarding exclusions in a policy was a statement of fact. **Similarly**, in <u>Anderson v. Deloitte & Touche</u>, 66 Cal. Rptr. 2d 512, 516–17 (Ct. App. 1997), the court

Cases applying the rule (see Ch. 11: Describe the Law)

Link between ideas = example

Relationship between ideas = similarity

concluded that inaccurate financial projections in an accountant's report were positive assertions of fact sufficient to create a triable issue of negligent misrepresentation. However, where a principal in an accounting firm stated his opinion as to the appraisal value of real estate, the court held that his statement constituted only his opinion because he was not an appraiser and had never represented himself as such. Neu-Visions Sports, Inc. v. Soren/McAdam/Bartells, 103 Cal. Rptr. 2d 159, 163–64 (Ct. App. 2000).

Relationship between ideas = difference

Application of law to facts (see Ch. 12: Explain the Analysis) – case analogies and distinctions

The defendants in Shafer and Anderson were professionals providing information regarding a matter about which they were known to have specific information. Similarly, Cramer was a professional who asserted the existence of a preferential admissions policy, a matter within his professional expertise. His situation is markedly different from the accountant's in Neu-Visions Sports, who asserted his opinion regarding appraisal value. As a recruiter, Cramer is presumed to know the admissions policies of the university that employed him. Even if his assertion that Eastern University's GPS program gave priority to its own graduates was an opinion, it was a statement related specifically to his profession. Therefore, like the statements in Shafer and Anderson, Cramer's statement should be regarded as a statement of fact rather than a statement of opinion

Relationship between ideas = similarity

Conclusion on issue A

Relationship between ideas = cause & effect

1st counter-argument & response

It is worth noting that recent cases concerning the distinction between fact and opinion in this context have concerned statements by defendants trained in recognized professions like law and accounting, not university recruiters. However, in Gagne, an earlier case, the court concluded that a statement regarding soil composition on a lot being tested for fill was one of fact even though the defendant had not held himself out as an engineer or geologist. The court so held because the defendant represented that he was in the business of testing soil for fill and because he had asserted his findings as fact rather than as a statement of his opinion. Gagne, 275 P.2d at 21. That

Relationship between ideas = difference

Cramer was a recruiter rather than an attorney or accountant thus is not likely to make a difference in the court's determination of this

Restated conclusion on issue A

question. A court is likely to conclude that Cramer's statement was a positive assertion of fact, rather than an opinion.

2ⁿᵈ counter-argument & response

It is possible, but not likely, that the court will regard Cramer's statement as an opinion rather than a statement of fact. His statement that Tyler would have "a better chance of getting into the GPS program as an Eastern Pacific graduate" is not as clearly factual as the attorney's statements regarding exclusions in the insurance policy in Shafer or the accountant's financial projections in Anderson. This may lead a court to view his statement less as a professional opinion constituting a statement of fact and more as an expression of his personal view of the situation. However, by telling Tyler that he would have a better chance of being admitted as an Eastern Pacific

Relationship between ideas = difference

Final conclusion on issue A

graduate, Cramer asserted the existence of a preferential admissions policy as a fact. Therefore, his assertion is likely to be regarded as a statement of fact, rather than his personal opinion.

Relationship between ideas = cause & effect

Appendix D

SAMPLE GRADING/CRITERIA SHEET
Exercise 14-A

_____

Name: _____

_____/5 **Statement of Thesis**: Ralph Watson is/is not liable for an assault upon a customer in Watson's grocery store committed by Claude Deemer, one of Watson's employees.

_____/10   **Rule:** An employer is liable for assault, an intentional tort, committed by an employee if
       ___/3   employee has propensity for violence
       ___/3   employer knew/ should have known of propensity
       ___/3   employer had employee work in public place
       ___/1   cite to <u>Tyus</u> or <u>Hersh</u>

_____/70   **Analysis**

___/23 **Propensity for Violence**
       ___/2   Thesis: Deemer did/did not have a propensity for violence
       ___/2   Rule: past behavior is evidence of violence. <u>Tyus</u> & <u>Hersh</u>
       ___/4   Case descriptions: In both <u>Tyus</u> & <u>Hersh</u>, customer and salesman, respectively, assaulted by employees who had been convicted of violent crimes

       ___/6 Application: propensity
              ___/2   Violent hockey play shows propensity
              ___/2   Suspended from play 21 days for unsportsmanlike conduct and fighting
              ___/1   Deemer's hockey league plagued with violence
              ___/1   Deemer's playing violent even by league standards

       ___/5 Application: no propensity
              ___/3   Unlike employees in <u>Tyus</u> & <u>Hersh</u>, had not been convicted of violent crime
              ___/2   Violent hockey play not necessarily indicative of violence off the rink

       ___/3 Reasoning (logic, coherence, clarity)

       ___/1 Conclusion

_____/26 **Knowledge of propensity**
       ___/2   Thesis: Watson did/did not know or should/should not have known of Deemer's propensity for violence
       ___/1   Rule: [reference to requirement given above]
       ___/4   Case descriptions: In <u>Tyus</u> & <u>Hersh</u> employer did not know and had no reason to know of prior conviction; had not seen employee behave violently

       ___/9 Application: knew or should have known
              ___/1   Watson was a hockey fan and season ticket holder
              ___/3   Watson had seen Deemer play in game in which he was suspended
              ___/2   Familiar with Deemer, team, and league; league plagued with violence
              ___/3   Distinguish <u>Tyus</u> & <u>Hersh</u> where employers did not know and had no reason to know of past violent behavior

___/6 Application: did not know or have reason to know
      ___/3   Unlike employees in <u>Tyus</u> & <u>Hersh</u>, Deemer has no criminal record
      ___/3   Unfair to require employer to equate violent hockey play with propensity toward violence off the rink

___/3 Reasoning (logic, coherence, clarity)

___/1 Conclusion

_____/21 **Public place**

   ___/2   Thesis: Watson did/did not hire Deemer to work in a public place
   ___/1   Rule: [reference to requirement given above]
   ___/4   Case descriptions: In <u>Tyus</u>, employee hired to work in service station with regular customer contact. In <u>Hersh</u>, employee worked in place not usually open to public.

   ___/5 Application: hired to work in public place
      ___/2   Deemer was maintenance worker in grocery store; contact with public inevitable
      ___/3   Deemer was cleaning trays in the produce department where customers were usually present and where assault occurred

   ___/5 Application: not hired to work in public place
      ___/2   Unlike employee in <u>Tyus</u>, Deemer not hired for position which required contact with public
      ___/3   Like employee in <u>Hersh</u>, contact with public only incidental to primary duties

   ___/3 (reasoning (logic, coherence, clarity)

   ___/1 Conclusion

_____/4 **Conclusion as to broad issue and reasons**

_____/11 **Organization and signposts**

_____/100 **TOTAL:**   Statement of Thesis (5 possible)   _____

                    Rule (10 possible)   _____

                    Analysis (70 possible)   _____
                    (Propensity   _____)
                    (Knowledge   _____)
                    (Public place   _____)

                    Conclusion (4 possible)   _____

                    Organization/signposts (11 possible)   _____

Suggested letter grade: _____

Appendix E

WRITING QUESTIONS PRESENTED

"This section alerts the reader to the specific issues addressed. It is therefore important to frame the issues as precisely as possible." A Practical Guide, page 225.

Precision requires three things: (1) stating the specific issue; (2) stating the relevant legal standard or rule; and (3) stating the legally significant or key facts. A Practical Guide, page 225.

The issues flow from the rules. In Exercise 14-A, for example, the rule, broken down into elements, is that a employer is liable for the intentional torts of an employee committed at the workplace and causing injury to a member of the public if (1) the employee has a propensity toward violence, (2) the employer knew or should have known of that propensity, and (3) the employer had the employee work in a place open to the public. Assume that elements one and two are at issue and that element three is given. Below is the process you would use to frame the questions presented.

Step 1

Begin your outline of the Questions Presented by listing the main issue and sub-issues.

Is an employer liable for his employee's assault on a customer at the employer's grocery store?

A.   Did the employee have a propensity toward violence?
B.   Did the employer know, or should he have known, of the propensity?

Step 2

List the significant facts under each issue and sub-issue.

Employee assaulted a customer at the employer's grocery store.

A.   Employee had no criminal record, plays in hockey league known for violence, suspended for fighting.

B.   Employer attended all games, including one in which employee was suspended.

<u>Step 3</u>

Combine steps 1 and 2.

Is an employer liable for his employee's assault on a customer at the employer's grocery store?

A. Did the employee have a propensity toward violence when he had no record of criminal violent behavior but played hockey in a league that was known for violent play and was suspended for fighting during a game?

B. If so, did the employer know or should he have known of the employee's propensity toward violence when he attended all games in which the employee played, including the game in which the employee was suspended?

In the previous example, there was one issue divided into two sub-issues. Here is an example of Questions Presented when there are three separate issues and no sub-issues.

I. Is a parent liable for damages to a school building under an East Dakota statute that imposes liability on a parent for harm intentionally caused by her child when the child placed a fire bomb in a car, intending to destroy the car, and the bomb's explosion destroyed both the car and a nearby school building?

II. If so, does the provision which limits the parent's liability to $7,500 in damages permit each of two plaintiffs, the owner of the car and the owner of the school building, to recover the statutory limit when the harm resulted from a single act?

III. Is a parent liable at common law for negligent supervision of a child who destroyed property with a fire bomb when the parent had knowledge that the child had occasionally started fires in the past when he was angry, the parent had obtained counseling for the child, and the parent relied on the advice of a child therapist regarding the child's condition?

You would have arrived at this final version by using the process described above.

<u>Step 1</u>: List the issues.

I. Is the parent liable under the statute for damages to the school building?

II. Can both plaintiffs recover the statutory limit?

III. Is the parent liable under common law for negligent supervision?

Step 2: List the significant facts under each issue.

       I.   The statute imposes liability on a parent for harm intentionally caused by her child; the child intentionally placed a bomb in a car in order to destroy it; the bomb also destroyed a school building.

      II.   The statute limits the parent's liability to $7,500; two plaintiffs were harmed by a single act.

     III.   The parent knew the child had started fires in the past, had obtained counseling, and had relied on a therapist's advice.

Step 3: Combine steps 1 and 2.

[Note that in this case, the parent's liability under the statute for damage to the car is a "given" because the child intentionally caused the harm. At issue is whether she is liable for unintended damages to the school building resulting from an intentional act.]

CREATING AN ELEMENTS & ANALYSIS CHART
See text Chapters 6 – 8, Statute & Cases in Teacher's Manual Exercises 5-F & 5-G

The following pages show how to combine elements of the charts in Chapters 6 through 8 of the text (Identifying Issues for Analysis, Common Law Analysis, and Statutory Analysis) into a single chart. This can be a useful exercise when students are preparing their first objective memorandum. In our experience, many students benefit from having to create such a chart as a pre-writing exercise because it requires them to process and organize all of the material they are working with, both facts and law. To create a good chart, students must pay special attention to the specific requirements of the elements of a rule and to the kinds of facts that are legally relevant to each element.

The following example is based on the shopkeeper's privilege statute and cases in Exercises 5-F and 5-G of this Teacher's Manual, and on the following facts:[10]

Charles Elmore, age 67, was shopping at Acme Supermarket, where he attracted the attention of a store security guard, 38-year old Alan Burke. Mr. Elmore has high blood pressure but is otherwise in good health. Burke is a part-time coach for a local high school fencing team.

Burke stopped Elmore as he was leaving the market and accused him of taking a bottle of aspirin, which Elmore had in his jacket pocket. Elmore explained that he bought the aspirin at a nearby drug store before coming to Acme. Burke told Elmore that he had been under surveillance and was seen taking the bottle of aspirin and "ditching" the box while shopping at the market. Elmore stated that he had been comparing prices but wanted to "clear things up." As he walked back into the market with Burke, Burke told the store manager, Nancy Walling, that he had detained a shoplifter and asked her to call the police. Burke led Elmore to the stock room in the back of the store and demanded that Elmore give him his jacket. When Elmore protested and attempted to leave the room, Burke grabbed Elmore's hands and handcuffed him to a large metal container, telling Elmore that he had to "preserve the evidence" until the police arrived.

Elmore told Burke that he had already swallowed three aspirin before Burke stopped him and asked Burke to count the tablets remaining in the bottle. He also said that Burke could find the aspirin box and his receipt in a trash can outside the drug store across the street. He repeated this story to Ms. Walling and a police officer when they arrived approximately 12 minutes later. Neither Burke nor Walling counted the aspirin or checked the trash can by the drug store. When the police officer left with Elmore, Walling searched the market for the aspirin box that Burke claimed Elmore had "ditched," but she did not find any such box in the market.

As a result of this incident Elmore sued Acme Supermarket for false imprisonment. Will the store be able to establish the shopkeeper's privilege in defense of Elmore's action?

A sample elements and analysis chart for this case appears on the following pages:

---

[10] The facts are based in part on *Colonial Stores, Inc. v. Fishel*, 288 S.E.2d 21 (Ga. Ct. App. 1981).

Element (§ 15-60-7)	Definition/Explanation of Element	Relevant Facts from Cases	Relevant Facts from Your Problem	Arguments Parties Can Make on Element
A storeowner	Includes agents & employees (§ 15-60-7)	Security guard(s) – Kovarik & Williams	Burke is store security guard	Not in dispute
detains	Actions, words, fear of force? – Kovarik & Williams	Physically taken to office, held in room with door locked – Williams	Burke stopped Elmore. Elmore went to stock room willingly. Burke physically restrained Elmore when he wanted to leave.	Not in dispute
a person thought to be shoplifting and				Not in dispute
against that person's will and	No action for false imp. if person consents to detention – Kovarik Physical force – Williams	Plaintiff signed consent form, did not ask to leave, wanted to "clear it up" – Kovarik Grabbed by the arm, taken to office, door locked -- Williams	Elmore went willingly when asked, to "clear things up." No consent form. Elmore later sought to leave, was handcuffed to a metal container. Elmore is 67 & has high blood pressure. Burke is 38 and a fencing coach.	Burke – Elmore agreed to come with him, expressed desire to "clear things up." B. only restrained E. when E. tried to leave; restraint only needed to preserve evidence until police came. Elmore – Posed no threat to stronger, younger Burke, and did not need to be physically restrained. Although initial detention was not against his will, it later became so when he attempted to leave.
that thought is reasonable and			Burke claims to have seen Elmore take item and discard package.	Burke – Had Elmore under surveillance; saw him take item and discard package. Elmore – Burke was mistaken; no evidence.

188

Element	Definition/Explanation of Element	Facts Relevant to Element – from Cases	Facts relevant to Element – from Your Problem	Arguments Parties Can Make on Element
person detained sues for false imprisonment **and**				Not in dispute
1 – a reasonable person would believe person was shoplifting **and**		Reports from co-workers – <u>Kovarik</u> Saw shopper place item in purse, not pay – <u>Williams</u>	Burke saw Elmore remove bottle from package, discard wrappings, place item in pocket, fail to pay.	Burke – See above re: reasonableness. Elmore – See above re: reasonableness.
2 – the detention was:				
a – reasonable in manner **and**	No "gratuitous or unnecessary indignities" – <u>Williams</u>	Threats, abusive language, sexism = not reasonable – <u>Williams</u>	Burke handcuffed Elmore to a metal container.	Burke – Physical restraint necessary because Elmore was attempting to leave and evidence would be lost. Elmore – He posed no escape risk given disparity in age and physical condition between Elmore and Burke. Physical restraint was excessive and humiliating.
b – reasonable in duration	No specific time; can be affected by manner of detention – <u>Williams</u>	10 minutes not reasonable when manner unreasonable (see above) -- <u>Williams</u>	Before handcuffed = not known. Time handcuffed until police arrived – 12 minutes.	Burke – held Elmore for the minimum time needed to preserve evidence until police arrived. Need for this manner & length of detention created by Elmore himself. Elmore - No evidence of any effort to ascertain the truth (e.g., look for wrapper). Unreasonable duration given manner of detention, Elmore's age & medical condition.